ASHE Higher Education Report: Volume 42, Number 1
Kelly Ward, Lisa E. Wolf-Wendel, Series Editors

Rethinking Cultural Competence in Higher Education: An Ecological Framework for Student Development

Edna Chun, Alvin Evans

Rethinking Cultural Competence in Higher Education: An Ecological Framework for Student Development
Edna Chun, Alvin Evans
ASHE Higher Education Report: Volume 42, Number 4
Kelly Ward, Lisa E. Wolf-Wendel, Series Editors

Cover image by © iStock.com/rusm

ISSN 1551-6970   electronic ISSN 1554-6306   ISBN 978-1-119-24465-3

The ASHE Higher Education Report is part of the Jossey-Bass Higher and Adult Education Series and is published six times a year by Wiley Subscription Services, Inc., A Wiley Company, at Jossey-Bass, One Montgomery Street, Suite 1200, San Francisco, California 94104-4594.

Individual subscription rate (in USD): $174 per year US/Can/Mex, $210 rest of world; institutional subscription rate: $352 US, $412 Can/Mex, $463 rest of world. Single copy rate: $29. Electronic only–all regions: $174 individual, $352 institutional; Print & Electronic–US: $192 individual, $423 institutional; Print & Electronic–Canada/Mexico: $192 individual, $483 institutional; Print & Electronic–Rest of World: $228 individual, $534 institutional.

CALL FOR PROPOSALS: Prospective authors are strongly encouraged to contact Kelly Ward (kaward@wsu.edu) or Lisa E. Wolf-Wendel (lwolf@ku.edu).

Visit the Jossey-Bass Web site at **www.josseybass.com.**

Printed in the United States of America on acid-free recycled paper.

The ASHE Higher Education Report is indexed in CIJE: Current Index to Journals in Education (ERIC), Education Index/Abstracts (H.W. Wilson), ERIC Database (Education Resources Information Center), Higher Education Abstracts (Claremont Graduate University), IBR & IBZ: International Bibliographies of Periodical Literature (K.G. Saur), and Resources in Education (ERIC).

Advisory Board

Contents

Executive Summary

CULTURAL COMPETENCE IS arguably one of the most critical skills that college graduates need for careers and citizenship in a diverse global society. Its importance is reinforced by the emergence of a minority majority American nation by 2042 and by the global nature of much professional work today. As a result, the urgency of the mandate to prepare college graduates for careers and citizenship in a diverse society requires focused efforts by colleges and universities to address the multiple, interlocking dimensions of diversity in the undergraduate educational experience. At stake is the relevance of a college education to students' ability to successfully navigate the complexities of multicultural working environments.

A number of colleges and universities have adopted inclusive excellence as a student-centered paradigm that addresses the synergy between diversity and quality in the intellectual and social aspects of the educational experience and fosters an inclusive campus environment. At the same time, however, most institutions have struggled to develop integrated and intentional approaches to addressing cultural competence in the curriculum and cocurriculum. The operationalization of cultural competence within the undergraduate experience remains an elusive and often neglected goal.

A key reason that colleges and universities have struggled with the attainment of cultural competence is the lack of a clear definitional framework that clarifies the meaning and implications for educational practice of such competence. Overlap with similar terms such as multicultural competence and intercultural competence has caused further confusion. Faculty steeped in an environment driven by disciplinary expertise may perceive cultural competence as a kind of "jargon" laden with politically correct overtones. The complexity of defining culture also poses a substantive challenge in moving from the predominant focus on nation states to an emphasis on the integral connection between culture and identity. Common conceptualizations of culture often fail to recognize the fluid, evolving nature of culture as it is redefined and contested by cultural members. In addition, the notion of "competence" itself is often disputed as a desired disciplinary outcome. As an example, the recent battle over the incorporation of a diversity requirement in the undergraduate curriculum at the University of California at Los Angeles (UCLA) referenced in this monograph reveals the contentious and ongoing nature of the academic debate relating to cultural competence and diversity learning outcomes.

By contrast, the helping professions including social work, counseling education, nursing, and medicine have identified the centrality of cultural competence in communicating with and working with diverse clienteles. A well-developed research literature in these fields offers substantive insight into how practitioners can operationalize cultural competence in their day-to-day work and has formed the basis of an emerging body of scholarship pertaining to the college or university environment.

Within the realm of higher education, cultural competence shares the inherent irony of the diversity rationale that has emerged from the legal reinterpretation of affirmative action by the Supreme Court. This reinterpretation requires that institutions of higher education demonstrate that white students receive educational benefits from policies that during the course of American history have reinforced white preference (Orfield, 2001). In fact, over the past 35 years, the court has moved from remedial, disparate-impact affirmative action designed to address historical discrimination to a nonremedial diversity rationale that establishes the educational benefits of diversity as the sole, acceptable legal basis for race-conscious admissions practices in higher education (Leiter & Leiter, 2011). From this perspective, cultural competence tends to focus on how white students grow and learn about other cultures while leaving unanswered the larger questions of what it means for students from underrepresented minority backgrounds on predominantly white campuses who may face assimilation pressures or pressures to conform to the dominant culture.

More often than not, the notion of cultural competence is stripped of its uncomfortable sociohistorical implications of inequality, social stratification, oppression, and privilege. The result is a bland and watered-down concept of cultural competence that often refers to international study, celebratory potlucks, and getting to know people from other nations.

In unpacking the meaning of cultural competence, we suggest an alternative term, namely, "diversity competence," that is more congruent with the range of educational experiences that occur on college campuses as well as the multilevel characteristics that make up the diversity spectrum. We offer a definition of diversity competence that encompasses the awareness, knowledge, and skills needed to communicate and engage with others who are different from oneself in interactions characterized by reciprocity, mutual understanding, and respect (Pope, Reynolds, & Mueller, 2004).

The lack of intentionality in campus diversity programs and practices is synonymous with "magical thinking" or the assumption that the attainment of a diverse student body automatically leads to realization of the educational benefits of diversity (Chang, 2007; Chang, Chang, & Ledesma, 2005). The monograph integrates a review and analysis of the literature coupled with the observations of 43 recent college graduates now engaged in professional careers or graduate study in a survey conducted for this monograph. The survey findings vividly illustrate the common disconnection between institutional diversity mission and the lived experiences of students on campus. For the most part, these graduates from different types of institutions had to seek out the diversity experiences they had and some of these experiences were purely accidental.

To address such disconnection, the monograph explores the application of a holistic, integrated ecological model to the development of cultural competence in the undergraduate experience. In this exploration, we note the frequent collision between macro-level, unequal social structures, and the everyday microcosm of student experiences that perpetuate systems of inequality through normative structures and social networks (Feagin, 2006). We introduce two prominent holistic environmental models for diversity learning outcomes: the Multicontextual Model for Diverse Learning Environments (MMDLE) (Hurtado & Guillermo-Wann, 2013) and the Culturally Engaging Campus Environments (CECE) model of student success (Museus, 2014). These nuanced models offer significant promise for systemic approaches to diversity learning outcomes.

The monograph then examines the common ground and points of connection between democracy citizenship learning outcomes and diversity competence. Studies confirm that democracy outcomes include a pluralistic orientation or the ability to view multiple perspectives and work cooperatively with diverse others as well as civic engagement and leadership skills. The goals of a liberal education provide a framework for developing democratic citizenship. Ideally, such an education provides a progressive learning continuum that moves from the self to others, culminating in cooperative work to achieve the common good (Musil, 2009).

The monograph offers an overview of the educational terrain for diversity through the development of a cohesive institutional approach across curricular, cocurricular, and service learning domains. Leading-edge examples of rubrics for the attainment of diversity competence provide ways to measure diversity awareness, knowledge, and skills. We also address the pivotal relationship between regional accreditation criteria and diversity competence. In this regard, the Degree Qualifications Profile (DQP) developed under the auspices of the Lumina Foundation presents a learning framework that includes the need for broad, integrative knowledge that addresses intercultural issues as well as civic and global competence that engages diverse perspectives.

Based on the research literature that substantiates the cognitive dissonance or disequilibrium arising from encountering difference, the monograph discusses the critical impact of diversity experiences on identity formation during the undergraduate years. This impact can be experienced by members of dominant groups and nondominant groups alike. Because of the critical time period for identity formation during college, we highlight approaches to structured intergroup interactions such as the Intergroup Dialogue Program (IGD) developed by the University of Michigan. IGD facilitates efforts to communicate across different social identity groups in the classroom, within the campus community, and in preparation for work in culturally diverse societies.

From an overall perspective, the monograph will serve as a resource for institutions seeking to provide an organizing ecological framework for the attainment of diversity/cultural competency in the undergraduate experience. The models and examples provided are applicable to a broad range of institutional types and settings. As a result, the monograph focuses on the ways in which colleges and universities can accelerate their progress in the development of an integrated campus ecosystem for diversity competence. The concrete recommendations for practice that conclude the book will assist institutional leadership, faculty, and administrators in developing systemic approaches to diversity competence during the undergraduate college years.

Foreword

A S STUDENTS PREPARE for life in an increasingly complex and global world, it is vital for colleges and universities to facilitate student development related to positive and productive interactions with people from a broad array of social and demographic contexts. In spite of the importance and even agreement that preparing students for operating in a diverse world is key, what is not always as clear is how to actually go about the work.

In this monograph, *Rethinking Cultural Competence in Higher Education: An Ecological Framework or Student Development,* authors Edna Chun and Alvin Evans provide readers with clear and thoughtful information about why cultural and diversity competence is important, how it can be integrated into the curriculum and other aspects of higher education, and how it contributes to student development. The strength of the monograph is in its specificity and comprehensiveness. Readers will find clear roadmaps to create programs and develop curriculum in addition to learning more about the importance of endeavors related to cultural competence. The authors provide clear definitions of different aspects of diversity that are informative.

The monograph is also helpful to readers in terms of providing different perspectives and a broad-based approach that looks at campus systems overall as well as societal contexts. Chun and Evans offer different views on diversity and cultural competence and tie them to different outcomes (e.g., democracy). The book goes beyond the "how to" of cultural competence by providing foundational information about why, in what ways, and to what end.

Chun and Evans take a unique approach in the writing of the monograph. Unlike many other editions in the series, the monograph relies on a combination of data from the authors' research in addition to an analysis and synthesis of the literature. The authors also integrate examples from institutions across the country. The result is a comprehensive volume that integrates theory, research, foundations, data, and practical approaches.

The monograph is sure to be of use to faculty, staff, and administrators looking for specific ideas on how to implement more intentional approaches to developing cultural competence. Too often a commitment to diversity is stated but not enacted. Some of the lag in action is from lack of clarity about how to develop students related to diversity outcomes and lack of support to pursue systematic approaches to developing cultural competence. Chun and Evans provide sage advice and multiple perspectives for how to garner institutional support to advance diversity education programs in addition to providing readers with multiple approaches that can fit different institutional contexts.

Throughout the series, as editors, we have been committed to pursuing topics related to diversity. The volume reads as a companion piece to Guthrie, Bertrand Jones, Osteen, and Hu's work on *Cultivating Leader Identity and Capacity in Students from Diverse Backgrounds*, as well as Museus' monograph on *Race and Racism* and *Critical Race Theory* by McCoy. Read together, these monographs provide a range of foundational information, critical perspectives, and strategies for a more intentional approach to developing diversity competence.

Kelly Ward
Lisa E. Wolf-Wendel
Series Editors

Acknowledgments

THIS MONOGRAPH IS dedicated to the memory of Alexander David Chun who exemplified in every way the attributes of diversity competence in embracing, valuing, and transcending all forms of difference in his relationships and professional work in the medical field. Alex designed the online survey of recent graduates that underpins the ethnographic research conducted for this monograph and brought his finely honed, critical research skills to the process. Alex taught us to question and refine our research assumptions and his nobility, courage, generous spirit, poetic creativity, and passionate sense of social justice will always serve as a compass and guide for us in our own journeys.

We especially thank Professors Kelly Ward and Lisa Wolf-Wendel for their foresight and encouragement on the need for a monograph on this important topic as well as their supportive guidance. We would like to express our gratitude to Professor Joe R. Feagin, Ella C. McFadden professor of sociology at Texas A&M University for his invaluable insights and suggestions that have immeasurably strengthened the monograph. We greatly appreciate the continuous, inspirational help of Professor Charles Behling, codirector of the Program on Intergroup Relations at the University of Michigan (retired), and his proactive outreach to recent graduates. We also would like to thank the peer reviewers for the many helpful and insightful suggestions that they provided.

We would like to express our appreciation to the dedicated professors who assisted us in contacting recent graduates and the survey participants who generously shared their time and perspectives related to recent college diversity experiences. We also thank Kimberly Thompson Rosenfeld for her responsive and skilled research assistance.

Finally, we express our deep gratitude to all the family, friends, mentors, and colleagues who have inspired us throughout the writing of the monograph and who continue to offer hope for a changed world.

The Politics of Cultural Competence in Higher Education

I realized that, although the university advertises diversity, diversity is still seldom seen on campus. I also realized that as a transracial adoptee, my checkbox says "Asian" while culturally, I am Scandinavian. My ideas and decisions are influenced by the Scandinavian culture. What does "diversity" even mean to the university?

Miranda, a transracial teacher and graduate
of a private Midwestern liberal arts college

M IRANDA, A TRANSRACIAL teacher who recently graduated from a small, predominantly white liberal arts college, questions the extent to which her institution's espoused commitment to diversity has been translated into reality. As a minoritized student, Miranda found the absence of faculty, administrators, and staff from nondominant groups at her college to be a matter of serious concern[1]:

I think that that's where the college struggles, to be honest. You can advertise that you have this percent of students of color... but when it comes to putting it into practice, the administration and all the higher ups were all Caucasian and the majority of my professors. I had two professors who were not. I am looking at our administration and our president, and our provost, and all of these people. There are no people of color really at all.

When I was looking at schools, I didn't think to ask about the diversity of faculty and staff. It makes a huge difference. I think that if the representation could have been there in the faculty and the administration that would help students relate better and especially students of color.

Unfortunately, the disconnection Miranda experienced between the institution's stated diversity mission and how this mission is reflected in the college's infrastructure and concrete practices is not uncommon within the realm of higher education. Evidence indicates that the alignment between espoused and enacted mission may be an important factor in student success (Museus & Harris, 2010). Few institutions have been able to bridge this gap to provide an integrated framework for diversity that fosters the learning outcomes and cultural competence students need to function effectively as citizens and employees in a diverse, global society. In fact, cultures of avoidance lead educators, administrators, and students to constantly evade acknowledgement of the realities of race and factors that advantage particular groups on campus (Harper, 2012a). Further, scholars have identified the absence of an authentic commitment to diversity and multiculturalism on college campuses as well as a superficial approach that fails to address the genuine inclusion of minoritized students (Jayakumar & Museus, 2012). Despite a substantive body of research that demonstrates the ways diversity can enhance learning outcomes (Chun & Evans, 2015), little evidence indicates that institutions of higher education have implemented a framework of policies and practices to implement diversity learning.

In this monograph, we address the development of cultural competence in undergraduate education through systematic efforts that create an integrated campus ecology for diversity. No blueprint exists for such development and no national policies guide this process. Because each campus represents a distinct ecosystem, we focus on research-based approaches that create an integrated, intentional framework for the implementation of diversity learning objectives and outcomes.

For the most part, the critical nature of cultural competence in the undergraduate college experience has been overlooked. Confusion and conflicting perspectives on the meaning and relevance of cultural competence abound. The lack of a clear definitional framework is a key reason that colleges and universities struggle with the operationalization of cultural competence. Terms like multiculturalism, diversity, inclusion, and cultural competence are often conflated into a "supra-diversity" concept that is both amorphous and ill-defined (Williams, 2013, p. 89). The notion of "competence" itself is loosely framed within the scholarly literature and fraught with conceptual and semantic landmines (see Spitzberg & Changnon, 2009). At times, it is equated with understanding, relationship development, satisfaction, effectiveness, appropriateness, and adaptation (Spitzberg & Changnon, 2009). At other times, competence is used to refer to a set of abilities and skills and can be equated with subjective evaluation (Spitzberg & Changnon, 2009).

More often than not, cultural competence is stripped of its uncomfortable sociohistorical implications of inequality, social stratification, oppression, and privilege. Well-intentioned members of the majority group appear reluctant to hear stories of pain, humiliation, and suffering experienced by marginalized groups in society (Sue & Sue, 2013). In addition, members of marginalized groups react strongly when their accounts of pain and discrimination are discounted (Sue & Sue, 2013). The result is a bland and watered-down concept of cultural competence that often refers to international study, celebratory potlucks, and getting to know people from other nations.

By contrast, a transformative paradigm for diversity encompasses the ethics and values of diverse communities, understands that multiple versions of reality are socially constructed and privileged, and recognizes power relations and dynamics in broad sociohistorical contexts (Nunez, Hurtado, & Galdeano, 2015). It offers the opportunity for systemic change through social justice efforts that address the need for disadvantaged or marginalized groups to gain increased opportunities for self-determination, empowerment, and voice (Goodman et al., 2004). Such a paradigm can infuse the efforts of universities and colleges to create a cohesive ecological approach to cultural competence.

Although relatively little progress has been made on operationalizing cultural competence in higher education, the helping professions, including social work, counseling education, nursing, and medicine, have integrated cultural competence within the realms of teaching, research, and practice. They have identified the centrality of cultural competence in communicating with and creating meaningful relationships with diverse clients as well as the relevance of such competence to patient outcomes. A well-developed research literature in these professions offers substantive insight into how practitioners can apply cultural competence in their day-to-day work. In fact, the multicultural competency frameworks and assessment methodologies developed by Derald Wing Sue and others in the counseling field have been adopted by student affairs professionals in higher education (see, for example, Pope et al., 2004; Reason & Watson, 2011).

Clear differences may exist on a campus in terms of the view of the importance of cultural competence, who is responsible for its attainment, and how it is to be attained. Aside from the widely accepted assumption that study abroad programs contribute to such competence, little agreement exists on a developmental model of learning leading to cultural competence (Twombly, Salisbury, Tumanut, & Klute, 2012). Because institutions of higher education desire legitimacy, colleges and universities often may exercise isomorphic behavior by copying other institutions in standard approaches to diversity and cultural competence due to the safety and comfort these approaches provide (Miller & Toma, 2011). In light of the social construction of legitimacy, such conservative practices can appear to invoke credibility and trustworthiness based upon the congruence between the institution's behavior and collective social beliefs (Suchman, 1995). Safer positions on contested issues such as cultural competence satisfy environmental pressures such as those deriving from widely accepted views of the existence of a color-blind, postracial society. Yet a dependency on sameness will no longer suffice, as the ways demographically diverse cohorts of students respond to campus environments are different from past responses (Harper & Quaye, 2009).

To complicate matters further, within each institutional environment, multiple constituencies, distinct subcultures, and decentralized decision making exacerbate efforts to crystallize a common, institutional agenda for attaining diversity learning outcomes and cultural competence. In large part, administrators, without consolidated input and direction by faculty, have driven diversity efforts. This bifurcation is problematic because faculty and administrators represent, in some sense, natural antagonists. The issues at variance between these two constituencies are the emphasis on discovery and disciplinary knowledge on the faculty side and the focus on sustainable competitive advantage and institutional growth in the face of resource constraints on the administrative side.

Faculty steeped in an environment driven by disciplinary expertise perceive cultural competence as a kind of "jargon" laden with politically correct overtones. Responding to cultural diversity through the curriculum and organization threatens the canon of knowledge espoused by dominant forces (Rhoads & Valadez, 1996). In addition, the canon suppresses border knowledge, or knowledge outside of the cultural mainstream that addresses the marginality that occurs through race, ethnicity, gender, age, and sexual orientation (Rhoads & Valadez, 1996). The lack of systematic attention to diversity learning outcomes across the faculty and administrative domains leads to disconnection, resulting in a plethora of piecemeal and often redundant activities. An additional challenge arises from the separation of faculty and staff reward systems within disciplinary or institutional silos, making it difficult to create more integrative learning experiences for students (Reynolds-Keefer, Peet, Gurin, & Lonn, 2011).

The result is that most campus diversity efforts are fragmented and localized within particular programs, such as initiatives for students of color in engineering, cultural houses to address campus life issues, or service-learning initiatives (Kezar & Eckel, 2005). These approaches are typically characterized by a lack of intentionality and even negligence and do not transcend departmental or program boundaries to address the needs of diverse students across the institution (Harper & Quaye, 2009; Kezar & Eckel, 2005). Such a laissez-faire approach is synonymous with "magical thinking" or the assumption that the attainment of a diverse student body automatically leads to realization of the educational benefits of diversity (Chang, 2007; Chang et al., 2005). In essence, weak institutions expect that students engage themselves and assume that the educational benefits of diversity will accrue automatically from the mere presence of demographic diversity (Harper & Quaye, 2009). Rather, diversity on college campuses is fundamentally about time-consuming and difficult work that needs to take into consideration the institution's context in shaping student learning as well as the dimensions and levels of campus climate (Milem, Chang, & Antonio, 2005).

From this perspective, institutional transformation in terms of diversity learning outcomes needs to be addressed systematically within the context of an institution's educational mission, historical legacy, and other contextually driven environmental factors. Drawing on the rich empirical literature on diversity and student learning outcomes, this monograph proposes a model for a holistic campuswide framework or ecosystem for the attainment of cultural competence through diversity learning outcomes. Given the heightened impact of a 4-year college experience on cultural competence as well as the growing body of longitudinal evidence on the educational benefits of diversity in this context, we focus on 4-year institutions, comprehensive master's institutions, and research universities in this monograph.

A Demographic Call to Action

Rapid demographic shifts in student enrollment reveal that the student body in higher education by mid-century will likely be minority majority. Consider the fact that between 1976 and 2012, the percentage of minority students more than doubled and has continued to increase, whereas the percentage of white students declined from 84% to 60% (National Center for Education Statistics, n.d.). In the span of just 2 years between 2009 and 2011, the number of black undergraduates grew by 8.5%, whereas the number of Hispanic and Latino undergraduates increased by 22%, with only 2.7% growth in white enrollment (Yeado, 2013). By 2060, the United States will be only 43% white. Since 1965, 40 million immigrants have arrived, with nearly 3 in 10 being Asian and half of them Hispanic (Taylor, 2014).

The population of Americans coming from more than one racial background has grown rapidly with 9 million respondents in the 2010 U.S. census reporting more than one race compared with 6.8 million in 2000 (Jones & Bullock, 2012). Although the numbers of multiracial students are increasing, higher education scholarship and practices addressing these new groups of students are both sparse and stagnant (Harris, BrckaLorenz, & Laird, 2014). Few practices have emerged to address issues of "identity dissonance" or the state of "in-betweenness" that arises among students whose parents come from different cultures (Garrod, Kilkenny, & Gómez, 2013).

The increasing diversity of the student body encompasses the primary dimensions of diversity that involve protected classes under federal executive orders and antidiscrimination laws regarding race, ethnicity, gender, age, sexual orientation, gender identity, and disability, as well as the secondary dimensions or socially acquired characteristics of diversity such as religion, socioeconomic status, parental education, geographic location, and military experience.

At the same time as college campuses grow more diverse, some young American adults may exist in a "cultural bubble" in terms of facility in another language, geographic awareness, and interactions outside of their own communities. A survey of 510 young American adults between the ages of 18 and 24 conducted by the National Geographic Society in 2006 reveals a surprising lack of geographical literacy by young Americans with only half of the participants able to identify the states of New York or Ohio on a map, only 38% able to speak a nonnative language fluently, 63% not able to find Iraq on a map of the Middle East, 75% not aware that a majority of Indonesia's population is Muslim, and 74% believing that English is the most commonly spoken language in the world, rather than Mandarin Chinese (National Geographic Education Foundation, 2006).

These findings underscore the urgency of preparing students with the knowledge, expertise, and skills necessary to work and participate as citizens in a global, multicultural society. Workplace transformation is taking place on a global platform at an accelerating place. An interconnected talent ecosystem has become increasingly specialized, diverse, performance driven, and team oriented (Bersin, 2012, 2014). Given the demand for college graduates who can expand the frontiers of research and knowledge, deliver new products, and serve diverse clients, cultural competence has become an indispensable facet of a college graduate's portfolio today.

A survey titled "Falling Short? College Learning and Career Success" by the Association of American Colleges and Universities (AAC&U) reveals significant disparities between the perceptions of students and employers related to readiness for future careers and the importance of diversity and intercultural learning outcomes (Hart Research Associates, 2015). The survey sample includes 613 students at private and public 2- and 4-year institutions and 400 CEOs and executives from private or nonprofit organizations. As shown in Table 1 below, one of the most surprising metrics is that fewer than two in five employers rated the following learning outcomes as very important:

TABLE 1
Learning Outcomes Less than Two in Five Employers Rate as Very Important

Awareness of and experience with diverse cultures and communities within the United States	37%
Staying current on global developments and trends	25%
Awareness of and experience with cultures and societies outside of the United States	23%
Proficiency in a language other than English	23%

Source: Hart Research Associates, 2015, p. 5.

Table 2 below reveals that despite the lack of emphasis by employers on these diversity and democratic learning outcomes, employers rated students as less prepared in the following areas than the students did themselves:

Only 21% of employers strongly agreed that all college students should gain intercultural skills and an understanding of societies outside the United States, whereas 57% agreed somewhat. By contrast, 87% of students felt that such skills were important. A similar gap was found between employer and student perceptions of the knowledge students should have of democratic institutions and preparation for citizenship in a democratic society.

TABLE 2
Employers and College Students Rate the Importance of College Learning Outcomes

Competency	Employer Rating	Student Rating
Awareness of and experience with diverse cultures and communities within the United States	21%	48%
Staying current on global developments and trends	18%	43%
Awareness of and experience with cultures and societies outside of the United States	15%	42%
Proficiency in a language other than English	16%	34%

Source: Adapted from Hart Research Associates, 2015, p. 8 5.

The lack of emphasis on intercultural understanding by employers is striking, given the fact that in the United States alone, there are more than 20,000 multinational companies, exceeding the number of companies in the Fortune 1,000 or the Fortune 5,000 (Fay, 2015). Moreover, the average U.S.-based multinational company generates roughly 45% of its revenue from countries outside the United States (Fay, 2015). The boundary between local and global has become blurred, as most companies compete in a global marketplace.

The survey also reveals that students agree with employers on the value of crosscutting skills of teamwork, communication, critical thinking, ethical decision making, and of applying knowledge in real-world settings. Ironically, however, in a global society and even within the United States all of these skills demand a high level of cultural competency, a recognition of cultural pluralism, and the ability to communicate effectively with individuals from diverse backgrounds and cultures.

Minimization of the value of cultural competence in higher education has resulted in glossing over its significance in the educational process and piecemeal attempts to infuse cultural competence into discrete aspects of the curriculum and campus life. At the institutional level, there is a striking dearth of information on how to attain it, ways to measure it, and the learning outcomes resulting from it. Although K–12 educators have devoted considerable research attention to multicultural education and other facets of the precollege experience of diversity, comparatively few resources address the systematic development of cultural competence and the associated diversity learning outcomes in the higher education environment.

The Veil of Color-Blindness

The prevalence of a color-blind racial ideology within the United States further obscures the pressing need for cultural competence. Such ideology is premised upon the notion of a postracial society in which race no longer matters as a marker of inequality. In this context, a surface-level multiculturalism creates ambivalence by celebrating and affirming difference, while avoiding privilege and racism as explanatory factors of disparities (Burke, 2013). A study in the counseling field finds, for example, that minimization of the existence of structural racism in the United States has been correlated with internalization of Eurocentric norms and significant variance in multicultural awareness (Neville, Spanierman, & Doan, 2006).

At the same time, a disturbing counterpoint of racist sentiments, discriminatory actions, and stereotypical remarks sharply contradicts the attainment of a postracial America. In this regard, a study of the journals of 626 white college students attending nearly 30 colleges and universities documents incidents that reveal a "thin veneer of apparent colorblindness" in performances by white actors in the frontstage or in public when diverse audiences are present (Picca & Feagin, 2007, p. xii). These performances are designed to make the actors appear nonracist but are contradicted by sentiments expressed in the backstage or in private when only white students are present. Although white Americans may indicate that they ignore racial characteristics at the micro level, many carry uncritically a white racial framing of society that takes shape in racial stereotypes, racist thoughts, and discriminatory inclinations (Picca & Feagin, 2007). Take the comments of a white student who worked as a cashier and reported her own reaction when a few Latinos spoke in a Spanish dialect and she could not understand what they were saying: "Then I asked myself, why are you even in this country if you don't know the language, why don't you go back to where you came from?" (Picca & Feagin, 2007, p. 128). Or consider the comments made to Middle Eastern students such as after the hijacking of planes on September 11, 2001. As one student recalls: "The Middle Eastern [student], Brad, was walking around like everyone else, when all of a sudden Chad said, "Hey hijacker! How are you?" (Picca & Feagin, 2007, p. 70). Another example is the statement by a student indicating that she was not comfortable having blacks in her room: "She told us she felt they were going to steal something from our room" (Picca & Feagin, 2007, p. 76).

On college campuses today, minoritized students are also experiencing the stress of social cohesion resulting from demographic transformation and a generalized lack of cultural awareness. Listen to the voices of students on university campuses who feel marginalized and isolated due to their race and ethnicity. Harvard University's Voices of Diversity (VoD) Project draws on interviews with at least 50 African-American, Latina/o, Asian American and Native American students at each of four universities regarding their on-campus undergraduate experiences related to their racial/ethnic background, sex, or both (Caplan & Ford, 2014). The report describes students' experiences of racist and sexist mistreatment that took shape in "micro-aggressions" or subtle, cumulative, and repetitive acts of marginalization and stereotyping.

A Latina senior quoted in the VoD study reports her reactions to discriminatory treatment: "I go nuts. I do . . . it hurts so much, so much, it's indescribable the way it makes you feel" (Caplan & Ford, 2014, p. 40). She goes on to say, "My whole body becomes hot, and your eyes automatically become glassy, because you just feel so inferior." An African-American male student describes his response to perceived mistreatment: "I don't feel that there is anything I can do. If I do anything physical, I'm in trouble. If I do anything through the wall, it's like, well he said, she said. What can I do? I feel useless. I'm being hurt by this person. It's messing with me emotionally" (Caplan & Ford, 2014, p. 40).

These painful realities underscore the continuing existence of stereotypes and exclusionary practices that can affect minoritized students on college campuses and that call for redoubled efforts to activate and operationalize institutional commitment to inclusion and cultural competence. Without institutional support and a psychological and social safety net, these students may suffer from a lack of self-efficacy and lack the ability to handle the barrage of academic and social challenges (Chun, 2013).

Inclusive Excellence and the Pathway to Cultural Competence

Within the last decade, the concept of *inclusive excellence* has been adopted as an organizing paradigm that addresses the social and intellectual development of students in diversity learning and competence. The Association of American Colleges and Universities advanced this concept to identify the synergy between diversity and quality—a synergy that is sometimes questioned within the walls of higher education. As an alloy of diversity and quality, inclusive excellence represents a compound that differs from its individual components, yet is stronger and more durable (Clayton-Pedersen & Musil, 2005). Far too often, diversity is assumed to dilute rather than strengthen quality such as in hiring processes when appointing authorities sometimes question whether quality will be compromised by consideration of diverse candidates.

Discussions of inclusive excellence often fail to emphasize that the focus of this aspirational framework is on student development. All four of the primary components of inclusive excellence are student centered: (a) student intellectual and social development; (b) purposeful use of institutional resources to enhance student learning; (c) consideration of the cultural differences students bring to the educational experience and that enrich the institution; and (d) a welcoming campus community that engages diversity in the service of educational growth and organizational learning (Clayton-Pedersen & Musil, 2005). Inclusive excellence also fosters engagement, an important factor in student success that influences the process of learning and the quality of educational experiences (Kuh, Kinzie, Buckley, Bridges, & Hayek, 2007). In this regard, research indicates that students with more diversity-related experiences are, on average, more engaged (Kuh et al., 2007).

Although a valuable conceptualization, the inclusive excellence model can be embraced rhetorically, without envisioning any type of fundamental change in prevailing ideologies, priorities, and processes. In fact, little evidence exists indicating that institutions of higher education have implemented the policies and practices necessary to make diversity work and to connect diversity experiences and courses to improve student learning (Goodman & Bowman, 2014). Taken seriously, inclusive excellence essentially demands a restructuring of unacknowledged and deeply embedded dominant discourses and institutional practices that permeate all levels of a college or university (Lee, Poch, Shaw, & Williams, 2012).

As a result, despite widespread acknowledgement of the value of the concept of inclusive excellence, colleges and universities have struggled in the operationalization of a cohesive approach to addressing the educational value of diversity across the various domains of the student experience. These areas include the curriculum, cocurricular activities, campus climate, residence life, experiences within the academic department, and opportunities for diversity interactions among faculty and students as well as among students themselves.

A comprehensive framework for inclusive excellence that acknowledges the value that diversity brings to undergraduate education naturally encompasses the goal of cultural competence as a key learning outcome. An Inclusive Excellence Change Model recognizes not only that diversity is an integral component of a strategy directed toward institutional excellence but also that institutions must make "concerted efforts to educate all students to succeed in a diverse society and equip them with sophisticated intercultural skills" (Williams, Berger, & McClendon, 2005, p. 3). As an exemplary practice illustrating this alignment, Emerson College (2015) identifies inclusive excellence and intercultural competence as both a value and performance indicator in the realization of its diversity vision.

One of the foundational challenges of inclusive excellence in a democratic, educational context is to create a climate of recognition and respect on campus as well as in relationship to external communities. Recognition is a pivotal concept bridging several disciplines, including political science and social psychology, and is integral to U.S. race relations (Feagin, Vera, & Imani, 1996). The refusal to see and recognize individuals from diverse groups as full human beings denies their place in the social world (Feagin et al., 1996). The cloak of invisibility has been a primary metaphor that captures the marginalization and exclusion of diverse individualities. Misrecognition or lack of recognition subverts the equality of social groups and the determination of individual identity. The failure to recognize others reproduces historical patterns of privilege, exclusion, and inequality in the educational institutions (Feagin & O'Brien, 2003). By contrast, cultural competence necessarily invokes recognition of the personhood of others, the uniqueness of individual identity, and respect for difference.

Purpose and Organization of the Monograph

The purpose of the monograph is to illustrate how colleges and universities can develop a systematic and sustainable approach to the development of cultural competence within the campus ecosystem. As a result, we do not seek to recapitulate the rather exhaustive literature on multicultural, intercultural, and cultural competence, but rather to address the following research questions:

- What is the meaning of cultural competence in the higher education context? How can the alternative term, diversity competence, add definitional clarity in terms of the range of student experiences within this context?
- What are the primary barriers to the attainment of diversity competence?
- What are the principal components needed to actualize a campus ecosystem for diversity competence in the undergraduate experience?
- How do research and emerging practices related to democracy learning outcomes pertain to the attainment of diversity competence?
- What promising models and exemplary practices exist for the creation of a campus environment that builds diversity competence?

The commentaries of 43 recent college graduates who participated in an online survey and follow-up phone interviews with 17 of these students illuminate both the deficits and positive attributes of campus practices related to cultural competence. These individuals graduated from 4-year institutions within the last 15 years and most are now employed in professional positions, with six enrolled in advanced degree programs. Their observations that are shared throughout the monograph shed light on the extent and quality of their undergraduate experiences of diversity as well as the impact of these experiences on their subsequent career trajectories. A summary of the demographics of the students surveyed can be found in Appendix A.

Given the lack of definitional agreement on what is meant by cultural competence, in the next chapter, we explore the complex, nuanced meanings of the term and identify commonalities and differences in the allied, often overlapping terms of multicultural and intercultural competence. In the process, we suggest an alternative term, "diversity competence," that is more congruent with the range of educational experiences that occur on college campuses as well as the multilevel characteristics that make up the diversity spectrum. We then share ways that institutions have addressed cultural or diversity competence as an integral part of the university or college mission.

The third chapter presents an ecological framework for the attainment of diversity competence and addresses the multiple dimensions of the campus environment that interact and contribute synergistically to the student's experience of diversity. Building on literature on the ecological model, the chapter explores the nested realities of social and institutional macrosystems and the collision of such systems with the day-to-day experiences of students in the everyday microsystems of dissonance and marginalization. The Multicontextual Model of Diverse Learning Environments developed by Hurtado Alvarez, Guillermo-Wann, Cuellar, & Arellano (2012) as well as the Culturally Engaging Campus Environments (CECE) model of student success (Museus, 2014) provide valuable frameworks that integrate multiple aspects of diversity within the lived campus environment. The fourth chapter examines democracy learning outcomes as one of the primary educational benefits of diversity that is specifically related to students' attainment of the diversity competence needed to function in a global society. The fifth chapter provides an overall perspective on the campus terrain for the attainment of diversity competency through components of a campus curricular and cocurricular inventory for diversity as well as an analysis of best practices that strengthen diversity competence. To further this analysis, in the sixth chapter, we explore the process of identity development as well as the impact of intergroup and cross-cultural contact on campuses. The chapter reviews representative models and major findings in these areas with a view to evaluating the degree to which students have the opportunity to engage in contact with other identity groups outside of their own. The seventh chapter concludes the monograph with recommendations for practice and an analysis of specific strategies and systems-based approaches that enhance the campus ecosystem for diversity competence.

To lay the groundwork for the monograph, we begin by unpacking the meaning of cultural competence as a diversity-learning objective within the context of the undergraduate experience.

Deconstructing Cultural Competence

Cultural competency is the child of diversity. So before we had never talked about diversity; we had talked about ... oppression and the white racial frame—whites sticking it to everyone else. And then we get into this phase of, "Let's embrace diversity and let's talk about diversity and let's hire and do this." But within that itself, people's perceptions of diversity in hiring practices and in housing, education, varies so much ... and then here we go with cultural competency, come the twin flavor of the century with diversity, but we are still at same place: we are still at a place that we have no idea what that means.

Martin, an African-American clinical professor and graduate of a Midwestern public research university

A N INITIAL CHALLENGE in defining cultural competence and its meaning in the undergraduate experience is to identify the inherent tensions laden in the term and to provide a clear, definitional framework pertinent to the higher education context. One of the main surprises in much of the literature on cultural competence is the extent to which the concept itself is ill-defined, overgeneralized, or assumed to be understood.

Consider how Martin, an African-American clinical professor in a prestigious Western private university who graduated from a predominantly white Midwestern research university, identifies the origins of cultural competence. He describes it as a "child of diversity" and as the "twin flavor of the century," which has supplanted overt recognition of oppression and the dominance of the white racial frame (Feagin, 2013). From this perspective, cultural competence has inherited diversity's vague and nonaccusatory emphasis that symbolizes good will and benefits to society as a whole, while failing to require meaningful change in conditions of social inequality (see Chun & Evans, 2015, for review; Kennedy, 2013).

Cultural competence shares the inherent irony of the diversity rationale that has emerged from the legal reinterpretation of affirmative action by the Supreme Court. Over the past 35 years, the court has moved from remedial, disparate-impact affirmative action to the nonremedial diversity rationale that established the educational benefits of diversity as the sole acceptable legal basis for race-conscious admission practices in higher education (Leiter & Leiter, 2011). In essence, this legal justification requires the university to prove that white students and all other students derive educational benefits from policies developed to address the long history of white preference (Orfield, 2001).

Like the educational benefits of diversity, cultural competence tends to focus on how white students grow and learn about other cultures while leaving unanswered the larger questions of what this means for minoritized students on predominantly white campuses who may face assimilation pressures or pressures to conform to the dominant culture (Chun & Evans, 2015). Such assimilation pressures can challenge and even destroy identity and marginalize the valuable knowledge and talent of diverse students who represent the very goals of cultural competence and social justice initiatives. Although cultural competence assumes the valuing of differences, it can also invoke normative white culture as the standard of comparison.

As we discuss in this chapter, culture is fluid, relational, and organically connected with individual identity. Whereas cultural competence acknowledges the existence of multiple cultures, from a historical perspective, in the United States, a Eurocentric cultural focus has determined the overriding cultural norms. The result has been a structured inequality of the playing field of culture and a hierarchical view of the "rightness" of the dominant culture.

In order to clarify the meaning of cultural competence, we first examine the complementary concepts of intercultural competence and multicultural competence in order to identify common elements and differences. Because there is considerable overlap among these terms, much work remains to be done in their conceptualization to arrive at clearer, more widely shared definitions (Van de Vijver & Leung, 2009). As noted earlier, our exploration is not designed to examine all aspects of the substantive literature on intercultural or multicultural competence but rather to highlight common themes and perspectives in order to arrive at a clearer understanding of the meaning of cultural competence. In light of this discussion, we then offer the alternative term of diversity competence as more consonant with the contemporary emphasis on the educational benefits of diversity and as more descriptive of the broad range of diversity interactions and learning outcomes that occur on college campuses.

Intercultural Competence

Cultural competence is often used interchangeably with intercultural competence, a term that has undergone significant evolution through critical scholarship. The concept of intercultural competence has arisen within the context of the field of intercultural communication. Despite the existence of numerous definitions and frameworks on intercultural competence, consensus has not been reached on its definition (Deardorff, 2011). Almost no empirical work exists that compares and tests the various models of intercultural competence that have been proposed (Van de Vijver & Leung, 2009).

In the early phases of scholarship in this field, culture was defined in terms of "nation state," and intercultural communication was studied from a generally interpersonal/microanalytic approach without attention to structural, power-based issues (Moon, 2010). Intercultural studies was grounded in equalized and neutral encounters between national group members, conceived as one-on-one relationships designed to equalize differences between the parties (Halualani & Nakayama, 2013). This initial emphasis brought into play an international perspective and the specific cultural attributes associated with nations or peoples.

Since 1996, however, the intercultural communication field has taken a critical turn with a shift in the meaning of culture to include other attributes of identification such as gender, ethnicity, race, sexual orientation, and social class (Moon, 2010). In addition, the intercultural field has moved away from the notion of shared of norms, values, and behaviors to an understanding of culture as a site of flux, struggle, and contestation (see Halualani & Nakayama, 2013; Moon, 2010, p. 38). Critical intercultural studies conceives culture as an ideological struggle involving historical power relationships and involving the relation between culture, identity, and power (Halualani & Nakayama, 2013). This focus is also critical to a conceptualization of cultural competence.

Intercultural competence emphasizes effective interaction between individuals who represent differing cognitive, affective, and behavioral orientations (Spitzberg & Changnon, 2009), and reflects the capacity of an individual to foster cooperative relationships with dissimilar others (Kim, 2009). In its most current formulation, it is conceived as culture-general (i.e., not specific to any culture) and context-general (i.e., applicable to any encounter between individuals of differing cultural or ethnic backgrounds) (Kim, 2009).

A number of theoretical models have been proposed for intercultural competence along with increasingly sophisticated efforts to develop and refine measures of such competence (Spitzberg & Changnon, 2009). Spitzberg and Changnon identify five model types of intercultural competence that are not mutually exclusive of each other: (a) compositional approaches that address the components of competence; (b) co-orientational models that emphasize concepts related to interactional approaches; (c) developmental models that identify progressive stages; (d) adaptational or more dyadic models that highlight the process of adjustment through the interdependence of actors; and (e) causal process models that provide a linear pathway verifiable with variables that support empirical testing (Spitzberg & Changnon, 2009). Three common themes in most Western models of intercultural competence are empathy, perspective taking, and adaptability (Deardorff, 2009). Yet some models may have depicted individuals as too rational, conscious, and

FIGURE 1
Intercultural Development Continuum

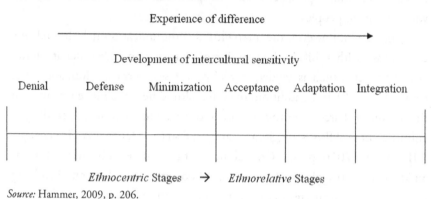

Experience of difference

Development of intercultural sensitivity

Denial　　Defense　　Minimization　Acceptance　Adaptation　Integration

Ethnocentric Stages　→　*Ethnorelative* Stages

Source: Hammer, 2009, p. 206.

intentional, without capturing the emotional components involved in intercultural interactions (Spitzberg & Changnon, 2009).

One of the best-known developmental approaches is the model of intercultural sensitivity (DMIS) developed by Bennett and others and later revised by Hammer as the Intercultural Development Continuum (IDC) (Hammer, 2009, 2012; Hammer, Bennett, & Wiseman, 2003). As shown in Figure 1, the IDC model identifies a continuum with five core orientations ranging from monoculturalism characterized by stages of denial and defense to the transition stage of minimization of cultural difference to the intercultural or global mindsets of acceptance and adaptation (Hammer, 2009, 2012; Hammer, Bennett, & Wiseman, 2003). This progressive continuum ultimately leads to cultural integration. Independent of these stages, the IDC also measures the cultural disengagement of the individual or the sense of disconnection or degree of alienation from one's own cultural group (Hammer, 2009).

At the beginning of the continuum, a denial orientation toward cultural diversity negates cultural differences and emphasizes the need for diverse others to fit into to historically derived values and practices. Polarization characterizes cultural differences in terms of "us" versus them, whereas a defense orientation sees these differences as threatening and divisive. The reversal orientation tends to overemphasize commonalities, masking a deeper appreciation of differences and the need to value diversity. Acceptance involves increased self-reflexiveness in experiencing both differences and common humanity, whereas adaption is characterized by a broadened repertoire of behaviors and frameworks that allow the individual to adapt to the cultural context (Hammer, 2009).

Another stage-based model of intercultural maturity is proposed by King and Baxter Magolda (2005) who sought to overcome the heavy reliance of multicultural competence models on assessment of individual attitudes as a proxy for competence. The developmental continuum developed by these researchers considers the cognitive dimension that includes complex understanding of cultural differences, the intrapersonal dimension of accepting and not feeling threatened by cultural differences, and the interpersonal dimension that involves functioning interdependently with diverse others (King & Baxter Magolda, 2005). In the intrapersonal domain, identity plays an influential role through the transformative processes of individuation or clear self-definition as well as in universalization or awareness of the universal aspects of human nature (Kim, 2009). Identity inclusivity enables individuals to transcend in-group, out-group categories and engage in associative, "communicative synchrony" (Kim, 2009, p. 56). Identity security enables individuals to feel secure enough in their own behaviors to engage with culturally diverse others (Kim, 2009).

A caution must be raised in terms of viewing the development of intercultural or cultural competence in stage-based terms. Linear, stage-based theories cannot address the complexity of human development, situational influences, and the diversity of developmental outcomes among individuals from differing cultures (Steenbarger, 1991). Nonetheless, these frameworks offer insight into how students achieve demonstrated outcomes around diversity issues through a process of growth and intercultural maturity (King & Baxter Magolda, 2005).

Multicultural Competence

Multicultural competence is another prominent, allied term that has gained significant attention in the research literature. This term has its origins in the multicultural education movement and was adopted in the early 1980s in the counseling psychology literature in a tripartite model of awareness, knowledge, and skills (Pope et al., 2004). The definition of multicultural competence is linked to the ability to work with and interact with others who are culturally different from oneself in meaningful ways (Pope et al., 2004).

Multicultural education arose as a school reform movement with a civic educational focus that took shape in the civil rights movement as an effort to overcome forms of unjust discrimination (Banks, 1995; Powers, 2002). In the view of its leading proponent, James A. Banks, multicultural education is driven by a moral and political logic aimed at reshaping social realities in alignment with a democratic vision (Powers, 2002). Banks conceptualized multicultural education as based on the concept that all students should have an equal opportunity to learn. As an educational reform movement, it represents a continuing process designed to create democratic ideals within schools (Banks, 1995). From this perspective, multicultural education consists of five dimensions: integration of content, the process of knowledge construction, prejudice reduction, a pedagogy of equity, and a school culture and social structure that is empowering (Banks, 1995).

Banks further identified five stages of ethnic development that include Anglo-Americans as well as other ethnic groups: (a) ethnic psychological captivity or internalization of negative beliefs about one's own ethnic group and characterized by ethnic self-rejection and low self-esteem; (b) ethnic encapsulation or ethnic separatism; (c) ethnic identity clarification or reduction of intrapsychic conflict to develop positive attitudes toward one's own ethnic group; (d) biethnicity or the psychological skills to function effectively in one's own and another ethnic culture; and (e) multiethnicity or citizenship identity within a pluralistic society (Banks, 1976).

Critical multiculturalism, like critical intercultural studies, seeks to transform educational institutions from "monolithic structures of power to democratic constellations" (Rhoads & Valadez, 1996, p. 9). Building upon this vision, Steinberg and Kincheloe (2009) identify a progressive typology of five levels of diversity and multiculturalism ranging from monoculturalism at the first level to critical diversity and multiculturalism at the fifth level. At the highest level, critical diversity addresses power, privilege, and domination and their impact on social and educational realities. This continuum explicitly recognizes the power of Whiteness as a cultural force and norm—a positionality and nonethnic space beyond history and culture (Steinberg & Kincheloe, 2009). When Whiteness is ignored or simply not acknowledged, race is seen as a factor affecting only nonwhites and the problems arising from difference (Steinberg & Kincheloe, 2009). Further, critical multiculturalism examines race, white supremacy, gender, patriarchy, and socioeconomic class both in terms of their interrelationships and as functions of each other (Steinberg & Kincheloe, 2009).

Within the context of the counseling professions, Sue and others (1998) have developed and fully elaborated a multifaceted framework of multicultural competence. This definitional framework captures the sociopolitical implications of Banks' theory and addresses 10 critical aspects of multiculturalism:

- Valuing cultural pluralism and acknowledging that our nation is a cultural mosaic
- Addressing social justice, equity, and cultural democracy
- Acquiring attitudes, knowledge, and skills to function effectively in a pluralistic democratic society
- Including characteristics of individual and collective diversity beyond race, class, gender, and ethnicity
- Celebrating contributions of our own and other cultures and exploring positive and negative aspects of our own and other groups' behavior that address history, conditions, and social realities over time
- Respecting and valuing other perspectives and worldviews without value neutrality. Investigating differences resulting from power and privilege
- Contributing to analytical thinking by incorporating conflicting bodies of information into sound perspectives
- Embracing change at individual, organizational, and social levels
- Acknowledging painful realities about oneself, one's social group, and society
- Achieving individual and social outcomes through inclusion, cooperation, and progress toward mutually shared objectives

Multicultural competence also involves understanding oneself as a racial/cultural being subject to biases, assumptions, and stereotypes, and the impact this may have on the counseling relationship (Sue et al., 1998; Sue & Sue, 2013). Individuals also need to understand the underlying preconceptions that may hinder cultural competence in an institution or organization (Sue & Sue, 2013). A multidimensional model for cultural competence occurs at the professional, organizational, and social level emanating from within concentric circles and involves a process of cultural conditioning at these three levels (Sue & Sue, 2013).

The literature on intercultural and multicultural competence yields valuable insights that illuminate the meaning of cultural competence within the domain of higher education. Critical intercultural studies and critical multicultural studies both address structural and institutional inequality and the interrelationship among characteristics of difference in relation to systems of power. To proceed further, we first need to unpack further the meaning of "culture" and "competence" as separate but complementary dimensions that illuminate the potential diversity learning outcomes of an undergraduate college education.

Rethinking Culture

Cultural competence necessarily brings into play the notion of culture and, by extension, concepts of the social group. Both philosophy and social theory typically have lacked a viable definition of the social group (Young, 1990). As Iris Young points out, the social group exists prior to individuals and in part, people's identities are affected by their group affinities. A social group, however, is constituted not by a set of shared attributes but by a sense of identity. Groups exist and are identified in relationship to other groups and their existence is fluid, shifting, and nonetheless, a reality (Young, 1990).

A number of major fallacies accompany predominant representations of culture that underscore the need for greater definitional clarity in addressing cultural competence. These fallacies tend to reify culture as a fixed entity rather than as a fluid and evolving construct shaped by cultural members:

1. *Culture is fixed, knowable, and certain.* Early anthropological scholars and cross-cultural psychologists viewed culture as certain, knowable, and apprehendable (Halualani, 2011). Descriptive and functionalist approaches to culture focus on comparison and classification and emphasize the beliefs, values, customs as well as material artifacts, instruments, and objects acquired by members of a social group (Halualani, 2011).

2. *Culture members necessarily share in a common collective identity associated with a given culture.* This view has the unintended consequence of squeezing individuals into broad categories that stereotype them and fail to account for individual uniqueness (Johnson & Munch, 2009). We can no longer resort to the simple premise that a given society or social group has a given culture (Eller, 2015). Because individuals do not control collective identities, the burden of adhering to such identities can result in a form of tyranny (Appiah, 1994, Johnson & Munch, 2009).

3. *The concept of cultural identity is synonymous with a given set of characteristics.* This perspective fails to account for the intersectionality of components of identity that include race, ethnicity, gender, sexual orientation, gender identity, disability, age, religion, and other distinct attributes. Individuals interpret cultural experiences through the interaction of a complex mediating set of these variables (Banks, 1998).

4. *All cultures have equal status and access to power and privilege in society.* Within societies, dominant cultures affect the views of individuals in terms of what is right and accepted and shape perceptions, attitudes, and behaviors. The term "ethnocentric monoculturalism" emphasizes the superiority of the dominant group in power that has been embedded within institutional culture and practices (Sue & Sue, 2013). Dominant groups tend to claim cultural universality and reinforce their position by bringing other groups under their dominant norms in a form of "cultural imperialism" (Young, 1990, p. 58). As a result, institutions need to acknowledge, rather than ignore, cultural differences and assist disadvantaged groups in preserving their culture against incursions by the dominant culture (Gutmann, 1994a).

5. *Cultural identities are not influenced by existing contexts, including political, structural, economic, and power-based realities.* This viewpoint ignores

the relationship between the individual and his/her environment, including the larger social forces of discrimination, racism, and oppression (Mendoza, Halualani, & Drzewiecka, 2002; Sue, Arredondo, & McDavis, 1992). Cultures are shaped by power relationships and the interplay between macro forces such as governmental, economic, legal, and institutional systems and micro interactions among different individuals and groups (Halualani, 2011; Roscigno & Wilson, 2014).

6. *Culture is disassociated by society from physical attributes.* Rather than understanding culture and physicality as opposites, society makes the physical "cultural" too by both culturizing the physical and physicalizing the cultural (Eller, 2015; Sahlins, 1976). The frequent association of all members of a racial group as having the same culture exemplifies this tendency.

7. *Membership in a cultural group is fixed rather than fluid.* The notion of "thrownness" introduced by the existential philosopher Martin Heidegger captures the notion of already having been a member of a given cultural group (Young, 1990). This "thrownness" does not predetermine whether individuals leave groups or enter new ones and how individuals relate to the identity of a given group (Young, 1990).

Heidegger's description of the contingent nature of being provides an apt conceptualization for cultural identity. It describes the contingent nature of being, as "thrown" within a given context, but still free to recreate itself and project itself toward its own potentiality-for-being (see Chun, 1985, for review). In essence, identities are not fixed but are projects, resulting from the interaction of contingent selves with determining structures (Chun, 1985; Mendoza et al., 2002; Young, 1990).

Not only is identity formed in relation to determining structures but also in relation to other individuals. Within a given context, relational dynamics are enabled or constrained through the medium of culturally prescribed and defined biases and expectations (Roscigno & Wilson, 2014). The notion of cultural capital introduced by the French sociologist, Pierre Bourdieu, establishes the focal elements of cultural interchange. Culture represents a distinct form of power with its own specific rules (Swartz, 1997). The field is the space in which cultural competence, composed of dispositions, norms, and tastes, is produced and given value (Winkle-Wagner, 2010).

Bourdieu uses the analogy of a poker game, in which the field has its own systems of valuation or rules that govern the criteria for entry, the cultural norms at play, whose voice is recognized, and the social relations in it (Winkle-Wagner, 2010). An individual's habitus or dispositions, tastes, and norms that represent the matrix of an individual's perceptions, actions, and appreciations can place unconscious limitations on individuals in terms of their career and educational goals (Perna, 2006; Winkle-Wagner, 2010).

As we explore the meaning of culture embodied in cultural competence, the perspective necessarily moves from the individual level to a larger view of society as a whole and the aspirations of a democratic society to include and value different voices and cultures. This democratic view, in turn, needs to infuse the development of cultural competence within the culture, climate, and organizational structures of institutions of higher education. In the third chapter, we further address this widening circle and the link between cultural competence and democracy learning outcomes in the undergraduate experience.

Unbundling Competence

The second part of the definitional equation of cultural competence is the attribute of competence. The notion of educational competencies moves away from the realm of knowledge for its own sake to the application of knowledge through specific competencies. Competency-based education models are outcomes-based approaches that provide skillsets through a learner-centered approach that is multidimensional, developmental, and contextual (Frank et al., 2010).

Competence is viewed as a changing, contextual construct that can represent a particular constellation of abilities that can take shape in different ways in different contexts (Frank et al., 2010). For example, competence-based medical education (CBME) addresses not only knowledge and skills but also values and attitudes and application of abilities in a clinical environment to obtain optimal results (Frank et al., 2010; Lobst, 2009). In clinical fields, such approaches provide the skills and competencies patients need, rather than relying solely on prefabricated sets of knowledge and data (Sherwin, 2011).

The characteristics of competency that can be drawn from the literature on competency-based education and applied to cultural competence include the emphasis on self-awareness, abilities, skills, dynamic contextual understanding, and the ability to navigate and negotiate in changing, complex situations. In this sense, cultural competence denotes a skill set that enables the individual to engage difference through interactions characterized by reciprocity and respect (Lee et al., 2012).

An Alternative Term: Diversity Competence

Given the need to contextualize cultural competence within the undergraduate educational experience, we suggest the alternate nomenclature of "diversity competence" as a synonymous, but less ambiguous and contested term for capturing the range of experiences gained through the educational process. The term "diversity competence" embraces research demonstrating that multiple types of diversity experiences influence learning (Goodman & Bowman, 2014). Experiences of diversity may not be associated with different cultures but rather with aspects of social identity. These experiences include "diversity interactions" or personal encounters that occur across dimensions of difference (Goodman & Bowman, 2014). The choice of this terminology embraces attributes of diversity that are not necessarily based on nationality or the attributes of national cultures.

Cox and Beale (1997) define diversity competency as "a process of learning that leads to an ability to effectively respond to the challenges and opportunities posed by the presence of social-cultural diversity in a defined social system" (p. 2). Because of the natural confusion that can result with internationalization as the primary focus of intercultural competence, diversity competence invokes a broader and deeper understanding of diversity that touches on both primary and secondary dimensions of difference.

Based on our extensive review of the meaning of terms that include intercultural competence, multicultural competence, and cultural or diversity competence, we paraphrase Pope, Reynolds, and Mueller's (2004) definition as the basis for diversity competence:

> *The awareness, knowledge, and skills needed to effectively communicate, collaborate, and engage with others who are different from oneself in meaningful ways through interactions characterized by reciprocity, mutual understanding, and respect.*

Commonalities in the definitions of intercultural, multicultural, and cultural or diversity competence include (a) recognition of cultural dominance and historical forms of exclusion that take shape through the channels of power and privilege; (b) recognition and respect for cultural differences; (c) a dynamic understanding of the contested and fluid nature of culture; (d) the connection of culture with identity and positionality; (e) the self-determination and self-affirmation involved in identity formation; and (f) the skillsets needed to engage and communicate with those who are different from oneself. These commonalities address the cognitive, behavioral, and affective dimensions of interactions. The term "diversity competence" differs from intercultural and multicultural competence in its emphasis on the full range of attributes that comprise diversity, whether associated with cultural differences or not. Diversity competence also invokes a broadened perspective consistent with the Supreme Court decisions that recognize the educational benefits of diversity. It reframes desired learning outcomes in terms of the multifaceted aspects of identity rather than an emphasis on nation states and race and ethnicity as the primary markers of difference.

As we further consider the dimensions of diversity competence within undergraduate education, we turn to examples of university and college mission statements that identify the value and importance of diversity or cultural competence and link diversity competency to the ability of graduates to navigate successfully in a global society.

Mission-Driven Statements of Diversity/Cultural Competence

Explicit references to cultural or diversity competency in a university's mission statement are rare. Consider the mission statement of Oberlin College, a private liberal arts college with a well-known professional school of music. This statement indicates the clear relationship of diversity to participation in the larger society:

> *Oberlin seeks a disparate and promising student body. Recognizing that diversity broadens perspectives, Oberlin is dedicated to recruiting a culturally, economically, geographically, and racially diverse group of students. Interaction with others of widely different backgrounds and experiences fosters the effective, concerned participation in the larger society so characteristic of Oberlin graduates. (Oberlin College, 2015, para. 3)*

Among the objectives of the undergraduate experience are nurturing students' social consciousness and environmental awareness and the development of skills and knowledge needed to navigate in a global society (Oberlin College). These objectives are interwoven with the development of "humane, thoughtful, and influential actors in the world" (Oberlin College).

Consider Dartmouth College's approach to transformative learning that emphasizes "Knowledge, Skills, and the New Meaning of Mastery" in an effort to prepare students for a rapidly changing global world of work (Dartmouth College, 2013). By taking learning beyond theory and the classroom, Dartmouth requires all undergraduates to develop competency-based objectives that complement curricular requirements through meaningful research, scholarship, and/or creative practice. Study abroad programs, personalized and hands-on learning, and working off campus contribute to students' readiness for a complex world of work. Educating beyond the degree represents an important educational objective designed to advance society through discovery and innovation and contribute to local, national, and global communities (Dartmouth College).

At the Massachusetts Institute of Technology (MIT), a taskforce on the future of education describes higher education as at an "inflection point" and notes that the Institute's educational role does not stop at the campus borders but includes a global community of learners ("Institute-wide Task Force," 2014, p. 4). The report includes five recommendations to transform pedagogy at MIT and five recommendations to extend MIT's educational impact to the world. The internal recommendations identify the need for an ecosystem that builds educational connections throughout the institute. Additional recommendations include expansion of the cohort-based learning community model to transform the undergraduate experience and development of an undergraduate service opportunities program to work on serious issues that challenge society. The recommendations to extend the institute's worldwide impact include using current, unresolved problems to spark global discussions and developing a more diverse group of learners for its MITx program that offers online courses and resources to students, individual, and organizational members outside of MIT. The MITx program also has the potential to develop new opportunities for global interaction for current MIT students ("Institute-wide Task Force," 2014).

Colleges and professional schools associated with the helping professions or whose graduates will have frequent community and client interactions are more likely to refer to cultural competence in their mission, vision, and values statements. Take, as an example, the identity and mission statement of the University of Washington School of Law that identifies the school's purpose as "Leaders for the Global Common Good" (University of Washington, 2014):

> *To accomplish our goals, we nurture a student-centered, culturally competent, and collegial community united by our commitment to sustainable excellence in achieving our vision and mission. . . . Our faculty members are the intellectual leaders of our community; they are culturally and intellectually diverse, distinguished in their respective fields.*

These examples position the need for diversity competence at the forefront of the student experience and provide insight into specific avenues for the attainment of this competence. Institutions of higher education are beginning to transform the undergraduate student experience to link in real time to a global audience of learners, provide competency-based education, strengthen experiential learning, and forge connections between knowledge and skills that will influence research, scholarship, and future careers.

Concluding Observations

As we have discussed in this chapter, the concept of cultural or diversity competence has eluded definition and has often been dismissed in academic circles as a politically correct, yet unnecessary appendage to the educational process. The belief that America has attained a color-blind, postracial society is contradicted by the persistence of exclusionary stereotypes, incidents, and behaviors on college campuses as shared in the examples in this chapter.

For the most part, colleges and universities have not grappled seriously with how to infuse diversity competence throughout the fabric of an undergraduate education. The decentralized nature of decision making, multiple power and authority structures, and the contrast between hierarchical administrative structures and the values of professional authority held by the faculty make change extremely difficult (Kezar, 2001). A focus on disciplinary-based knowledge attainment can overlook the competencies students need to function effectively as professionals in a diverse, global society. As critical forms of intercultural and multicultural scholarship emphasize, connection with the core American values of equal access, opportunity, equality, and autonomy also needs to include recognition of the prevalence of antidemocratic forms of power and privilege (Giroux & Giroux, 2004). The profound impact of social-historical forces in terms of issues of inequity and power has influenced both individual and group identity formation (Williams, 2013).

At the same time, we have seen considerable overlap and confusion in the use of the concepts of multicultural, intercultural, and cultural competence. Common elements in these terms need to be clarified in order to arrive at a starting point for consideration of their meanings and definitions in higher education. As discussed in this chapter, a critical view of culture moves from a focus on nation states to an emphasis on the integral connection between culture and identity. A more nuanced understanding of culture needs to take into account its fluid and dynamic nature and the fact that culture itself is not always characterized by "sharedness" but can be contested and redefined by individual members. Further, consideration of culture necessarily invokes considerations of power, privilege, and inequality and the hierarchical view of culture arising from dominance of Eurocentric perspectives. The neutralization of culture and its "unproblematized description" as a given set of characteristics of a group by virtue of their geographic location hinders the understanding of culture as an "ideological struggle" among competing interests (Halualani & Nakayama, 2013, p. 6).

Finally, the term "diversity competence" appears more representative of the different domains of the college and university experience and the multiple aspects of diversity that include both primary and secondary dimensions. It is consistent with the Supreme Court's emphasis on the educational benefits of diversity in the affirmative action cases over the last 35 years. This legal emphasis has given rise to an extensive literature on different dimensions of the educational experience that contribute to diversity learning outcomes.

In the next chapter, we address the development of an integrated ecosystem or ecological framework for the attainment of diversity competence in the undergraduate experience, building on recent research on the educational benefits of diversity. Findings from our student survey shared in the next chapter shed light on the urgent need for a systematic and coordinated approach to diversity competence in higher education that transcends disciplinary silos and bureaucratic divides in order to prepare students with the knowledge, skills, and mindsets needed for their future careers in a diverse, interconnected global society.

An Ecological Framework for Developing Diversity Competence

I don't think the university was diverse or the culture embraced diversity. It certainly didn't live up to its mission, but I did see a lot of people working towards that. It [the mission] certainly wasn't operationalized through some behavior that people demonstrated. . . . Whether that was racial slurs, writing on people's cars, or homophobic remarks off campus or even violence inspired by racist beliefs or homophobia—I would see faculty, staff and leadership take a stance on that and take action to really uphold the mission to have a diverse student body and diverse learning experiences.

Seth, a gay, white student affairs administrator and graduate of a Midwestern public college

SETH'S OBSERVATIONS ON the culture of his predominantly white public college demonstrate the impact on students when a campus ecology does not embrace diversity. Despite the lack of a systemic approach to diversity at his university, Seth notes the well-intentioned efforts of certain faculty and administrators to respond to racial slurs and homophobic remarks on an ad hoc basis. The absence of an integrated ecosystem for diversity places the onus on the good will of individuals to resolve difficult issues and uphold the institution's espoused mission.

Seth's account is not atypical and underscores the need for intentional and focused attention to how students experience diversity throughout the entire continuum of the undergraduate experience. Such an integrated perspective includes not only curricular requirements but also classroom experiences, faculty–student relationships, behavioral modes of interaction, opportunities for interactional diversity with individuals from different social identity groups, cocurricular and service-learning programs, athletic programs, and residential living arrangements (Bowman, 2011, 2012; Chun & Evans, 2015; Jayakumar, 2008). In this chapter, we draw together major themes in the research literature to delineate the principal elements of an institutional ecology for diversity competence.

An ecological framework for diversity competence addresses the ways in which multiple dimensions of the campus environment interact and contribute synergistically to the student's experience of diversity. As noted earlier, the definition of diversity within an ecological framework is necessarily broad based and encompasses both the primary dimensions protected by federal executive orders and antidiscrimination law including race/ethnicity, gender, age, disability, sexual orientation, and gender identity as well as the secondary dimensions that include religion, socioeconomic status, veteran's status, and other acquired characteristics. Because diversity is often equated solely with race and ethnicity, a more comprehensive orientation integrates complex understandings of forms of difference in terms of how these forms interrelate and contribute to institutional dynamics and educational context (Chang, 2013).

An example of the powerful impact of secondary aspects of diversity is shared by Chris, a biracial male graduate of a small, private Eastern liberal arts college. Chris elected to join the ROTC program on a campus that did not support military training and this programmatic decision affected the process of identity formation. He explains how this lack of institutional support affected him:

It did challenge my sense of identity. There was not strong support for the ROTC program, especially my freshman and sophomore year. I really had to push back to say who this is who I am, it is part of my life; and my college had to accept it. . . . But, the college wasn't the most supportive; they didn't have their own programs; however, there was one at a different campus. I had to push for my rights as student to take the class. I think it really made me hunker down and believe in who I am and what the program offered which really made me believe in it more. The pushback really actually helped push what I wanted and made me realize who I was and who I wanted to be.

The tension between the lack of support for this aspect of identity by his college and his own desires forced Chris to clarify his own life goals and career trajectory.

As a result, a holistic perspective on diversity competence necessarily invokes an intersectional lens that considers how multiple aspects of an individual student's identity shape and create unique perspectives (Museus & Griffin, 2011). Intersectionality brings the positionality of the individual into view and counters the fixed, essentialist notion that all members of a given group have a single perspective with the acknowledgment that individuals have multiple, overlapping identities (Kezar, 2002). Because society is structured along binaries of black and white, rich or poor, determining which of the multiple aspects of identity others react to can be an uncertain proposition (Ladson-Billings, 2013).

The goal of intersectionality analysis is not focused on the creation of a hierarchy of oppressions but instead offers an understanding of how both privileged and marginalized aspects of an individual's identity produce experiences that are distinct from those who may share certain aspects of identity but not others (Museus & Griffin, 2011). For example, a gay Latino student may experience more or less oppression than his white male gay counterparts (Museus & Griffin, 2011). However, oppressions can work in tandem with each other to compound the effect of inequality, a phenomenon described as "multiple jeopardy" such as with the intersection of race, class, and gender (see for example, Collins, 1993).

Attributes of Campus Diversity Experiences

Turning from the multiple elements of diversity that coalesce in social identity, we now explore several attributes of campus diversity experience established in the research literature. Despite a substantive body of recent research relating to the educational benefits of diversity, knowledge about specific diversity initiatives and interventions, how they work, and their impact is at a nascent stage (Hurtado, Griffin, Arellano, & Cuellar, 2008). Viewed from an ecological perspective, many factors, both internal and external can enhance or detract from the impact of the educational experience on students' diversity learning (Chang, 2011).

Findings on the educational benefits of diversity reveal that the impact of diversity on student experiences is both conditional and indirect. Diversity learning outcomes are conditional because they depend on the characteristics of the individual student, the differences in the interpersonal environments they experience, and the presence of differing within-campus environments that provide the opportunity for participation or membership (Clarke & Antonio, 2012; Pascarella, 2006). These outcomes are indirect because they operate through students' experiences and result from interactional, environmental, or structural factors such as the level of cross-racial student interaction (Chang, 2011; Gurin, Dey, Hurtado, & Gurin, 2002).

Yet structural diversity alone will not lead to the attainment of an integrated framework of diversity experiences without greater levels of student engagement across multiple domains including curricular diversity and cross-racial interaction (Bowman, 2013a; Chang, Astin, & Kim, 2004; Clarke & Antonio, 2012; Denson & Chang, 2009; Sorensen, Nagda, Gurin, & Maxwell, 2009). Structural diversity has been described as a necessary, but not sufficient condition for diversity learning outcomes that must be leveraged through intentional practices to attain the benefits of diversity (Clarke &

Antonio, 2012; Gurin et al., 2002). Take, for example, a study of 19,667 students in 227 4-year institutions, which found that students on campuses that had higher levels of cross-racial interactions reported greater gains in openness to diversity with the ability to accept different cultures and races (Chang, Denson, Sáenz, & Misa, 2006). In addition, a longitudinal study of 8,615 first-year students from 49 public and private institutions further confirmed that structural diversity does not guarantee frequent intergroup interactions (Bowman, 2013a).

Although existing research often treats organizational environments as a unitary phenomenon, a network analysis reflects the different ways that students experience the environment in several important respects: (a) how student learning for diversity is activated through patterns of interrelationships among individuals; (b) how students perceive the campus environment based on their social identity; and (c) how institutional policies and practices that affect structural components of student relations are related to diversity learning outcomes (Clarke & Antonio, 2012; Hurtado, Alvarado, & Guillermo-Wann, 2012; Hurtado & Guillermo-Wann, 2013; Rankin & Reason, 2005). From this perspective, the racial dynamics among differing student populations is not monolithic and differentially influences the ability of students in these groups to optimize the benefits of diversity (Clarke & Antonio, 2012). For example, contrary to common assumptions that Asian Americans may be exempt from discrimination, one study reveals that Asian Americans and multiracial students report higher frequencies of discrimination than some other racial groups (Hurtado & Guillermo-Wann, 2013). As a result, when campuses are able to obtain balanced, structural conditions, the mutual enhancement of diversity resulting from educational processes is achieved by bridging across diverse groups such as through cross-race tie formation (Clarke & Antonio, 2012).

These insights from the research literature reveal that the educational benefits of diversity are not automatic, require institutional planning, and operate conditionally depending on students' own social identities, level of awareness, and willingness to engage across difference. In the course of this chapter, we discuss some of the important structural and environmental conditions on campus that can facilitate diversity learning.

Application of the Ecological Model to Campus Environments

The ecological model has proven to be a valuable framework for student development in higher education (see, for example, Arnold, Lu, & Armstrong, 2012; Dey & Hurtado, 1995; Hurtado et al., 2012; Renn, 2004; Renn & Arnold, 2003). Based upon the theory of developmental psychologist Urie Bronfenbrenner (1976, 1977, 1979), the ecological paradigm presents a topological depiction of the educational environment that places the learner at the center and consists of a nested set of structures, like a Russian doll, each contained within the next (Bronfenbrenner, 1976, 1977, 1979, 1995). From micro to macro levels, the learning environment consists of:

- the microsystem experienced by the learner that includes the setting and individual roles,
- the mesosystem or system of microsystems that encompasses interrelationships and interactions,
- the exosystem or external communities and social structures that do not directly involve the learner but that affect the mesosystem,
- the macrosystem that includes political, social, economic, legal, and policy contexts, including culture and ideology that affect social structures (Bronfenbrenner, 1976, 1977, 1979, 1995).

In later iterations of the model, the chronosystem of time plays a prominent role in increasingly broad time intervals throughout this continuum (Bronfenbrenner & Morris, 2006). Bronfenbrenner's progressive framework addresses the process of continual adaptation through the person-process-context-time model that includes the individual, the relation of the individual to the environment, the context in which the individual develops, and the sociohistorical milieu (Bronfenbrenner, 1995). Figure 2 illustrates the application of the ecology model to a campus environment (Renn 2003, 2004; Renn & Arnold, 2003):

The multidimensional ecological framework captures the reciprocal, dynamic interrelationship between the student and the campus environment,

FIGURE 2
Applying the Ecology Model to a Campus Environment

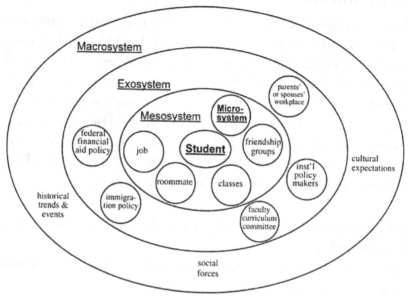

Source: Renn, 2003, 2004; Renn & Arnold, 2003.

with students having the capacity to shape their interpersonal environment, whereas institutions, in turn, provide the potential for individual transformation (Chang, 2011; Dey & Hurtado, 1995). The interlocking dimensions of diversity in the student experience involve (a) multiple levels of context; (b) the interdependence of components, actions, and behavior; (c) a phenomenology-based approach in terms of how people's experiences shape reactions and consequences; and (d) the principle of person-environment adaptation (Bond & Haynes, 2014).

The Clash Between the Macro and Micro/Meso Levels

The existence of multiple levels in the campus ecosystem does not mean that these levels interact harmoniously. In fact, the collision between the macro level of unequal, stratified social structures, and the everyday micro level of student interactions can cause painful experiences of marginalization and dissonance within the campus ecology. At a macro level, institutions have continually created, recreated, and reproduced systems of inequality through normative structures and social networks (Feagin, 2006). Systemic racism is an explanatory framework that addresses how race has shaped American society through the unjustly gained political and economic power of the white majority, persistent resource inequality, and ideologies of privilege (Feagin, 2006). The reproduction of systemic racism within the predominantly white university is communicated personally, structurally, and ideologically through subtle and overt behaviors, attitudes, and practices that persist in the 21st century (Feagin et al., 1996).

Recent racist incidents on college campuses are a reminder that college campuses have been the sites of exclusion and discrimination and those vestiges of such discrimination remain. The admission of African-American students into most predominantly white institutions did not occur on a significant scale in both the North and the South until the 1960s (Feagin et al., 1996). The full desegregation of higher education remains a goal rather than a reality in some geographic areas (Feagin et al., 1996). Overt racist behavior persists on college campuses in the backstage and is regularly reported in the press when it appears on the frontstage (Picca & Feagin, 2007). For example, the chant sung by members of the Sigma Alpha Epsilon (SAE) fraternity at the University of Oklahoma calling for the lynching of blacks contradicts the predominant view that racial discrimination on college campuses is no longer a serious problem. University of Oklahoma president, David Oren, addressed the "institutionalized culture" of racism in the SAE fraternity, indicating that the students had learned the chant at a national leadership conference of the fraternity that has a membership of 15,000 and then adopted it for initiation ceremonies (Svrluga, 2015).

Consider the way the sociohistorical macrostructures of inequality imploded on the daily experiences of Martin, the African-American clinical professor cited earlier, as an undergraduate in a public research university:

> *It challenged my sense of identity because once again I was reminded of what the world thought of me, you know those historical*

perceptions of race. In high school and middle school it's like a constant trying to prove oneself that you had value and you were as smart as the mainstream. And I thought college would be the one place it would stop. Because you got here so you expected everyone here to have the "it" factor to make it. I found himself fighting for four more years to prove [myself]; it sort of made me bitter. I would say it strengthened me in terms of my resolve; but I wouldn't say it was like a positive strategy. But I have seen some of my peers, where they rebelled, they either dropped out or some of them dropped out. But the others who made it, it was like building up of a callous on the hand, that's what it did for me.

Take the account of Anthony, a white male doctoral student with a mild form of autism spectrum disorder, who describes how conservative peers at a small, white, liberal arts college attended by many wealthy students, treated him. His fellow students refused to shake his hand or even touch him:

Powerful experiences can be good, and powerful experiences can be bad. I interpret powerful as something long lasting. It was an experience I had with some college Republicans. . . . When I was talking with some of them, they simply couldn't relate to the idea of not having enough food or not having clothes. They were automatically assuming that disability meant disease. It seemed to be rooted in some sort of 1950s understanding.

My bachelor's program really sucked, it was quite isolating. . . . By and large, I had a rather cruddy experience there. It is very difficult to think of something truly positive. It certainly contributed to my idea of expanding diversity in the workplace.

Anthony sums up his view of how diversity should have been integrated within the context of the college experience:

Diversity in my mind it is a matter of experiencing cognitive dissonance in such a way that it does challenges horizons of understanding. In this case my very presence and their reaction to me was one that challenged my concept of education.

Nonetheless, students also have the capability of affecting the larger social macrosystem of inequality as a direct result of their experiences with diversity during their college years. Our interviews suggest that even a single diversity mentor can have a life-changing effect on student perspectives and career choices. For example, Seth changed his major to sociology as a result of his deepened understanding of power and privilege gained as an undergraduate and brought this increased awareness to his work in student affairs at a large western research university.

Holistic Environmental Models for Diversity Learning Outcomes

Given the relevance of the ecological paradigm to the educational process, we now focus on two prominent ecological models that address diversity learning outcomes and student success: the Multicontextual Model for Diverse Learning Environments developed by Hurtado and others (Hurtado et al., 2012; Hurtado & Guillermo-Wann, 2013) and the Culturally Engaging Campus Environments (CECE) model of student success (Museus, 2014). These models describe a layered, multidimensional ecological approach to diversity but offer a somewhat different perspective from each other. The model developed by Hurtado and others focuses on the creation of a campus environment that yields the educational benefits of diversity, whereas Museus' model identifies factors that enhance cross-cultural engagement and promote student success. Both models can be seen as complementary and mutually reinforcing.

As shown in Figure 3, the Multicontextual Model for Diverse Learning Environments (MMDLE) places social identity at the center, centers on dynamics within meso-level spheres of interaction such as in the classroom and curriculum, and includes the exosystem of the community and macrodynamics of sociohistorical and policy contexts. Further, the MMDLE identifies the interrelationships between the campus diversity climate, educational practices, and three educational outcomes: habits of mind for lifelong learning, competencies for a multicultural world, and student achievement and retention (Hurtado et al., 2012; Hurtado & Guillermo-Wann,

FIGURE 3
The Multicontextual Model for Diverse Learning Environments

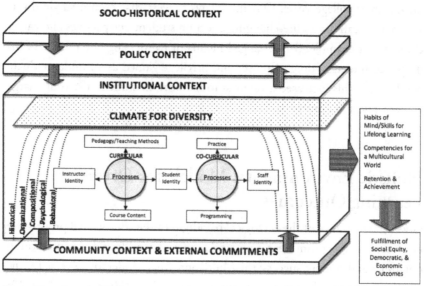

Source: Hurtado et al., 2012.

2013). Using this model, the Diverse Learning Environments (DLE) campus climate survey instrument that was piloted in 2010 at 14 institutions assesses multicultural competencies through factors that measure pluralistic orientation, civic engagement, redressing social inequalities, awareness of privilege and critical consciousness and action (measuring how often individuals challenge their own and others' biases) (Hurtado & Guillermo-Wann, 2013).

The second environmental model, the CECE, offers a new theoretical perspective designed to build on existing frameworks and serve as a tool to promote the success of diverse student populations (Museus, 2014). Although the CECE model includes both white and minoritized students, it is based primarily on research relating to students of color (Museus, 2014). As a result, the nine factors that characterize culturally engaging campus environments are weighted toward definitions that address the cultures of diverse students within the campus ecosystem. The first five factors focus on campus environments relevant to the background and communities of diverse students (Museus, 2014; Museus & Yi, 2015):

1. Cultural familiarity or the extent to which students can interact with faculty, staff, and peers from common backgrounds
2. Culturally relevant knowledge or the opportunity to sustain and increase knowledge of cultures and communities of origin
3. Cultural community service or the ability to give back to and transform students' cultural communities
4. Cross-cultural engagement or purposeful and positive interactions with diverse peers
5. Culturally validating environments or the extent that institutions and educators convey that they value diverse identities and cultural backgrounds

The four remaining indicators relate to how campus environments respond to the cultural norms and needs of diverse students (Museus, 2014; Museus & Yi, 2015):

6. Collectivist cultural orientations or the proposition that students who experience institutional environments based on more collectivist orientations are more likely to succeed
7. Humanized educational environments in which institutional agents develop meaningful relationships with students
8. Proactive philosophies and practices of engaging with student populations
9. Availability of holistic support that provides access to faculty and staff who can offer help or connect students with resources and information

The model also considers the impact of external influences such as family and financial background and precollege inputs as well as individual influences such as the sense of belonging, academic dispositions and motivation, and academic performance (Museus, 2014).

To provide further perspective on how internal, contextual elements of a campus ecosystem for diversity can constrain or catalyze the creation of a holistic learning environment for diversity, we next explore the impact of four leading factors in the institutional exosystem for diversity: institutional culture and climate, physical environment, the impact of diversity leadership, and organizational learning processes.

Campus Culture and Climate

Campus climate and culture undergird and permeate student experiences of diversity. Campus culture can be understood as an invisible tapestry that serves as an interpretative framework for understanding events and actions (Kuh & Whitt, 1988). It draws upon the deeply embedded values, norms, and assumptions that are not easily changed and crystallize an organization's distinctive character (Peterson & Spencer, 1990; Schein, 2010). The strong sense of control and ownership that faculty, administrators, and students feel over culture and climate is unique to higher education, resulting in a virtually intractable culture that often is slow and resistant to change (Williams, 2006). The psychological and behavioral barriers that impede inclusion within the campus psychosocial environment have received increased attention in light of the invisibility of subtle, second-generation forms of discrimination that affect faculty, administrators, and students (see, for example, Chun & Evans, 2012; Evans & Chun, 2007; Smith & Wolf-Wendel, 2005).

The construct of climate refers to a more transient, fluctuating yet often complex environmental phenomenon that can be "chilly" or inhospitable to individuals from nondominant groups (Smith & Wolf-Wendel, 2005). It also invokes the shared meaning that community members attach to policies and practices including behaviors that are rewarded and supported (Schneider & Barbera, 2014). As such, it refers not only to the psychological climate that members of an institution experience but also the objective climate that can be measured by patterns of behavior and formal activity (Peterson & Spencer, 1990).

Climate is a particularly important dimension of the ecology of diversity because experiences of prejudice and discriminatory experiences have been shown to negatively affect the sense of belonging, adjustment, and persistence of students from both dominant and nondominant groups and white students (Museus, Nichols, & Lambert, 2008). A holistic conceptualization of a campus climate for diversity indicates that it is a multidimensional environmental construct that includes five primary subcomponents: (a) the institution's historical legacy of exclusion or inclusion; (b) structural or compositional diversity of faculty, staff, and students; (c) psychological climate composed of attitudes and perceptions between and among racial/ethnic groups; (d) behavioral climate as characterized through intergroup campus relationships and (e) organizational diversity or the structures, policies, and processes that pertain to diversity (Hurtado et al., 2012; Hurtado & Guillermo-Wann, 2013; Hurtado, Milem, Clayton-Pedersen, & Allen, 1998, 1999).

Research findings over the past five decades have established *campus racial climate* as a critical aspect of the institutional context that shapes students' attitudes and experiences of the educational benefits of diversity (see, for example, Feagin et al., 1996; Harper & Hurtado, 2007; Hurtado, 1992; Jayakumar, 2008, Ward & Zarate, 2015). Campus racial climate specifically refers to the attitudes, behaviors, and expectations community members have regarding issues of diversity, race, and ethnicity (Hurtado et al., 2008; Hurtado et al., 1999). Perceptions of institutional climate impact the job satisfaction of faculty from nondominant groups and survivors of such environments can face hostile circumstances and continued marginalization (Levin, Jackson-Boothby, Haberler, & Walker, 2015). A hostile campus climate with negative cross-racial tensions can lead to students' low perceptions of their ability to navigate in a diverse world (Hurtado & DeAngelo, 2012).

Take, for example, how Tracey, a white female graduate of an isolated, predominantly white Western research university, describes the racial climate at her institution. Her university represents, in her words, "a hard place to be a black and Latina student," with less than 8% minorities among the student body and only 2% black students. This lack of demographic diversity and a conservative white environment severely affects the learning process. In the criminology/sociology program, she recalls how the presence of conservative and even hostile students had a chilling effect on the class participation of African-American students:

> *Unfortunately, we don't have a ton of racial diversity, it makes up less than 8% of our campus…There were about 15 black students in my graduating class and I had classes with several of them. They oftentimes didn't feel very comfortable speaking up in class because our degree program is a mixed criminology/sociology program. There are some very, very conservative and almost hostile*

students in the program ... that's just by and large the experiences that continue to happen here on our campus. It really provides kind of a chilling effect for African-American students and other under-represented minority students. We have a larger Native American population. And they also feel really uncomfortable speaking up in class because of this chilling effect.

As Tracey's narrative illustrates, inadequate attention has been devoted to the role of cultural perspectives in campus racial dynamics and the ways to promote sustained and productive cross-cultural engagement (Museus, 2008).

In the effort to gauge the impact of campus climate on student interactions, intergroup relations, and student learning outcomes, more than 90 campus climate survey instruments have been developed dating back to 1985, including five instruments that focus on multicultural competencies (Hurtado et al., 2008; Hurtado & Guillermo-Wann, 2013). As the literature on climate indicates, campus climates are often more alienating than involving and more hostile than encouraging (Smith, 1990). In fact, diversity is far too often a condition characterized by alienation and seen as a problem rather than as central to the purpose of the institution (Smith, 1990).

Organizational culture has particular bearing on whether diversity reaches beyond the institution's mission statement and strategic plan to affect underlying mindsets, values, and actions. A comparative study conducted by the American Association of State Colleges and Universities involving 420 members in 12 groups of institutions found that the one dominant feature characterizing high-performing institutions was institutional culture and an inclusive approach to promoting student success that engaged the entire campus (Howard, 2014).

Given the interrelated dimensions of an institution's culture and climate, the concept of *cultural integration* is particularly valuable in creating an ecosystem for diversity competence. This concept addresses the overall integration of students' cultural backgrounds and experiences with the academic and social realms of student experience and has been linked to positive educational outcomes (Museus et al., 2012). Although cultural integration has generally focused on the experiences of racial and ethnic minority students within campus subcultures, it also provides an important lens for understanding how white students conceptualize their identity and integrate this understanding with campus diversity experiences and learning.

As a case in point, Vince, a white male security guard and emergency management technician, became aware of the implications of his own white identity as a sociology major on a predominantly white, geographically isolated Western university campus:

> *I was a typical white male, I learned how responsible my group is for everything else that everybody else has gone through. So everything isn't as nice as people like to think. We have had a lot of impact on the negativity that everybody else has experienced. . . . I didn't know all the details. I didn't know to what extent those effects still had on certain groups of people. I certainly knew the general points of history. It was easier to kind of put aside and not think about. Learning about the intricacies brought it to the forefront in terms of my consideration of everything.*

Tinto's theory of academic and social integration postulated that students must first separate from groups such as family with which they were associated, undergo transition, and incorporate or adopt the normative values and behavioral patterns of the new group (see, for example, Tinto, 1988). By contrast, cultural integration refers to the continuing engagement and evolution of students' cultural identities in the academic setting and the extent to which academic, social, and cultural aspects of student lives are reflected across the educational continuum (Museus et al., 2012). An intercultural perspective emphasizes the institution's influential role in validating cultural backgrounds of minoritized students and including both collective and individual cultural influences regardless of whether these occur inside or outside the classroom (Museus, 2014).

The Campus Physical Environment

Another important component of campus ecology is the physical milieu that creates the setting for social interactions (Bronfenbrenner, 1979). The link between the functional and symbolic aspects of physical environments on campus can influence behavior such as when nonverbal messages contradict verbal messages (Strange & Banning, 2001). For example, a campus president can speak about the welcoming nature of the campus to diverse students, while defamatory graffiti on buildings sends a different message (Strange & Banning, 2001).

Space as an experiential reality is at the center of interpersonal relations and is a critical aspect of race relations on a campus (Feagin et al., 1996). Many spaces on predominantly white campuses are racially charted and delimited, although often in subtle ways (Feagin et al., 1996). Minoritized students often describe such spaces by social rather than physical characteristics, such as "hostile" or "alien" or "unwelcoming" (Feagin et al., 1996). For example, one African-American parent driving through a predominantly white state university described the campus in chilling language: "The first time I rode through it looked like Ku Klux Klan country....State University...just looked cold when I rode there" (Feagin et al., 1996, p. 15). He added that he had already heard that the campus was racist and this feeling was confirmed by driving through the campus for only a half an hour (Feagin et al., 1996). A study of 24 biracial or multiracial students from three undergraduate-focused institutions found space—both private and public—to be a critical psychological dimension of fitting in (Renn, 2000). Students described the need for public spaces with others who shared their interests and private spaces in which to define their own identities such as through academic projects, journal writing, and conversations with trusted friends (Renn, 2000).

Diversity Leadership

Diversity leadership is a driver and differentiator in the institutional exosystem for diversity that determines whether or not cultural change takes place or whether the status quo prevails. It is a distinctive form of leadership that addresses diversity issues, challenges distinctive power arrangements, and adapts to the changing global environment (Aguirre & Martinez, 2002, 2007). In essence, it requires committed action by members of dominant and nondominant groups alike. As President Emeritus Bob Suzuki of Cal Poly Pomona explains (B. Suzuki, personal communication, June 23, 2015):

> Based on my own experience in promoting diversity, I believe it is critically important for the top administrators, from the president on down, to lead such efforts and to keep reminding everyone of their importance. And as I see it, promoting the cultural competence of students is just one dimension. There are many other important dimensions of diversity that include the recruitment of faculty, staff and administrators of color, efforts to help students of color succeed in the STEM disciplines, diversifying counseling center staffs, and many other areas of an institution.

One of the distinct challenges for leadership in creating a systemic approach to diversity learning is the bifurcation between faculty and administrative spheres in terms of operational values, employment conditions, and role expectations. The bureaucratic model of administration with its emphasis on centralized power, orthodoxy of fundamental values, and authoritarian control of subordinates (Chesler, Lewis, & Crowfoot, 2005; Tuchman, 2009) contrasts sharply with core faculty values that emphasize academic freedom, autonomy, and functional independence (see Chun & Evans, 2012, for review). The development of more inclusive, "revolutionary" leadership models that focus on empowerment, social responsibility, and collaborative management (Kezar & Carducci, 2009) remains a work in progress. More frequently, different microclimates exist within an institution, and the implementation of inclusive practices varies considerably among campus divisions and departments.

From a structural standpoint, the lack of diversity in leadership positions influences decision-making in the university and mirrors the racial stratification of American society (Chun & Evans, 2012). The predominant whiteness of leadership raises the question of institutional responsiveness to rapid demographic shifts in student populations (Hurtado & Alvarado, 2015). Governing boards are mainly composed of white men with women comprising 28.4% of public institutions' governing boards and 30.2% of independent college and university governing boards (Schwartz, 2010). Racial and ethnic minorities represent only 23.1% of members on public governing boards and 12.5% of members of independent college and university boards (Schwartz, 2010). More than four-fifths of board chairs are men (Schwartz, 2010). Because the board is the public face of an institution, without a critical mass of at least 30%, the contributions of underrepresented groups will not be sufficient to get beyond tokenism (Schwartz, 2010).

For over a quarter century from 1986 to 2011, the demographic profile of college presidents has remained unchanged (Cook, 2012). The typical profile of a campus president is a white male, married with children, Protestant, with a doctorate in education, and having served in his current position for 6 years (Cook, 2012). The representation of minority college presidents increased only 5% over a 25-year span from 8% to 13% (Cook, 2012). When historically black colleges and minority-serving institutions are excluded, only 9% of presidents are minorities (Lederman, 2012). Women made greater headway in attaining the presidency during this time period, increasing their representation from 10% in 1986 to 26% in 2011 (Cook, 2012).

A study of 27 college presidents who were known to have made significant progress on a diversity agenda revealed that in addition to structural initiatives such as mission statements, diversity strategic planning, and diversity councils, these presidents in essence relied on a networked, horizontal perspective of leadership that could be compared to a supportive spider web of support (Kezar, Eckel, Contreras-McGavin, & Quaye, 2008). The six nodes of the spider web include faculty, administrators, staff and especially student affairs personnel, boards, students, and external organizations (Kezar et al., 2008). Strategies invoked by presidents to advance the diversity agenda include human resource strategies that involve collaborating with faculty on the curriculum, hiring and mentoring of diverse faculty, interacting with and learning from students, working with student affairs educators, obtaining board support, and creating external networks (Kezar et al., 2008). Given the fact that institutions are "democratic microcosms" of society and reflect the ideological divisions of a more diverse society, presidents may find that they are circumscribed by pressures from numerous constituencies on sensitive issues such as racial diversity and multiculturalism (Freedman, 2003, p. 11).

The role of the chief diversity officer (CDO) has received increased attention over the past decade with at least 60 institutions that have engaged in reframing the senior diversity administrative role (Williams & Wade-Golden, 2013). CDOs represent the only exception to the largely white-dominated senior leadership positions in higher education, with 70.8% of these positions held by African Americans and only 12.3% by whites (King & Gomez, 2008). The diversity strategic plan is an important structural element that enhances institutional accountability, communicates the importance of diversity both internally and externally, assesses progress toward multiyear goals, and ensures that institutional resources are devoted to diversity programs (Evans & Chun, 2007). CDO positions, however, may have little formal authority to hold individuals accountable who do not report to them and often need to operate through persuasion, symbolic power or the ability to bring financial or human resources to the table (Williams & Wade-Golden, 2013).

Because diversity leadership challenges homogeneity, it may not be compatible with organizational culture in higher education and requires "radical, fundamental change" (Aguirre & Martinez, 2007, p. 36). Given the need for organizational will and political power to galvanize the change process, the mantle of diversity leadership needs to be assumed by members of dominant and nondominant groups whose influence will help overcome diversity resistance (Chun & Evans, 2009). One of the most powerful levers for accomplishing such change is organizational learning, as we shall discuss in the next section.

Organizational Learning as a Catalyst for Change

Within the context of the campus ecosystem, organizational learning presupposes that change in the conditions for diversity must occur at the institutional level (Smith, 2004). Such learning is focused on the process of the diversity effort and how it unfolds within an institution (Smith & Parker, 2005). It leads to greater institutional effectiveness because it relates to the institution's core work, is driven internally but considers external community influences, and requires both intentionality and continuity (Smith & Parker, 2005).

In other words, transformational change cannot be left to individual actors or the occasional training program. Instead, it requires that a critical mass of individuals within the institution operate in new ways leading to the establishment of infrastructures that support learning and new norms and habits (Argyris, 1994). Such large-scale changes in practice can be initiated by a small number of individuals (Rynes, 2007). Yet to be successful as a sustained and deliberate institutional priority, such learning needs to be supported by presidents, boards of trustees, and through shared governance processes.

The Campus Diversity Initiative (CDI) undertaken at 28 independent California colleges and universities between 2000 and 2005 is a prominent example of how institution-level change designed to build campus capacity for diversity can be advanced through organizational learning (Clayton-Pedersen, Parker, Smith, Moreno, & Teraguchi, 2007). This initiative incorporated a strong evaluative approach and recognition that institutions must address all levels of organizational culture to make progress on a diversity agenda with careful attention to everyday attitudes, practices, and beliefs (Clayton-Pedersen et al., 2007).

The ADVANCE grants of the National Science Foundation (NSF) are another example of how organizational learning can be tied to institutional transformation for diversity. The grants are designed to increase the representation of women in academic science and engineering careers through systemic institutional approaches to overcome factors that hinder women's advancement unrelated to individual ability such as organizational constraints and implicit and explicit bias in evaluative processes (NSF, n.d.). In particular, the Institutional Transformation Catalyst track focuses on strategy implementation and self-assessment, and the Partnerships for Learning and Adaptation track is focused on providing a larger-scale environment for strategy implementation through networked adaptation and learning (NSF, n.d.). With an investment of over $130 million in more than 100 institutions of higher education, ADVANCE programs emphasize proactive recruitment processes, search committee training and development, and organizational learning initiatives (NSF, n.d.).

These examples offer insight into the ways in which organizational learning can infuse diversity within the campus ecosystem through intentional processes that lead to new norms and overcome behavioral and organizational constraints to diversity progress.

Concluding Observations

The ecological model introduced in this chapter serves as a viable and dynamic framework for conceptualizing the development of student diversity competence through the multiple domains of the undergraduate experience. The strength of the ecological perspective lies in its emphasis on the reciprocal and dynamic interrelationship of the learner with the environment as well as the intentional practices needed to support diversity learning.

Yet the ecological model also highlights the potential clash between macro-level social structures and day-to-day student experiences within the micro and meso domains. The reproduction of social inequality within the university environment is evident in narratives we have shared, whether it be through unwelcoming cross-racial interactions, stereotypical expectations in the classroom, or exclusionary administrative structures. As these interviews reveal, the clash between individual identity and the prevalent university culture can affect the individual's self-concept and self-esteem as well as his or her future career trajectory. The disappointment expressed by students who had hoped their institutions would embrace the value of diversity reflected in admissions materials underscores the wide gap between the university's espoused mission and lived reality on the ground.

Recent graduates in our survey sample who served in roles like residential advisor requiring contact with diverse students and resolution of complex issues reported that they were able to draw on these experiences in their subsequent work environments. Several of the interviewees cited the influence of faculty role models in providing them with a deeper understanding of diversity and facilitating discussion about difficult issues in the classroom. White students coming from homogenous neighborhoods shared examples of how their awareness and understanding of diverse groups and of whiteness itself was expanded through the presence of structural diversity on their college campuses.

As discussed earlier, however, studies confirm that the mere presence of structural diversity will not facilitate diversity learning outcomes without the benefit of intentional practices that foster and leverage interaction across difference (Sorensen, Nagda, Gurin, & Maxwell, 2009). A college campus is not a unitary environment and is experienced differently by individual students, depending on demographic background, type and level of interaction with diverse peers, selection of courses and major, residential or nonresidential status, involvement in cocurricular activities, experiences with faculty, and many other factors. The complexity of these variables indicates that experiences of diversity will differ markedly on a given campus and that context is critically important. For these reasons, the development of a holistic, ecological approach requires attention to the multiple layers in the MMDLE and the intersection of experiences across different levels.

Most important, as colleges and universities seek to address their role in society as engines of democracy, new knowledge, and change, they serve as a crucible for individual student development that can influence the larger forces of social transformation. From this vantage point, the capacity students gain to value and appreciate difference, to understand sociohistorical patterns of privilege and inequality, and to work collaboratively with diverse colleagues in team-based structures represent essential learning outcomes connected to the liberty and justice aims of a democratic, pluralistic society. Given the ecological framework discussed in this chapter, we next focus on democracy learning outcomes as one of the primary educational benefits of diversity. Democracy learning outcomes are recognized by professional associations and leading educational organizations as a significant aspect of a liberal education.

The Educational Benefits of Diversity and the Link to Democracy Outcomes

It [my undergraduate experience] prepared me naturally to respect differences . . . and just having that kind of respect, I find helps me to get along with coworkers from other backgrounds. It could be something small. For example, I have an Indian colleague who fasts on Mondays and has dietary restrictions on Thursday. In Japan, that kind of thing can be made fun of . . . I come from a background where everyone is expected to behave in a rather similar way. So after being exposed to diversity in college, and meeting with different people with different religious beliefs, different family backgrounds and cultural backgrounds, I feel that I am prepared to recognize difference and I need to also have respect for difference as well.

> *Mai, an Asian administrator and graduate of a private Midwestern liberal arts college*

IN THIS CHAPTER, we focus specifically on a critical aspect of the educational benefits of diversity: democracy learning outcomes that prepare students for a diverse workplace and citizenship in a global society and enhance their diversity competence. To attain a global perspective, definitions of learning need to evolve from the association with value-free rational knowledge derived from abstract reasoning to a broader view of learning or wisdom that transcends cultures and time periods and is situated within a multicultural and global world (Kezar, 2005).

Mai, a Japanese native who attended a selective liberal arts college known for its legacy of social justice activism, contrasts her college's diversity environment that fostered interaction across differences with her cultural upbringing in Japan. The welcoming environment on campus helped her in her subsequent career in a multicultural, international nonprofit organization. By contrast, a hostile campus climate with negative cross-racial tensions can lead to students' low perceptions of their ability to navigate in a diverse world (Hurtado & DeAngelo, 2012). As Mai's narrative illustrates, a campus ecosystem for diversity can be the springboard that prepares students for future careers, yielding a more complex cognitive and affective understanding of difference and providing the practical competence to navigate with confidence in a diverse and interconnected world.

Types of diversity learning outcomes documented extensively in the research literature include the following areas: (a) prejudice reduction and enhancement of cross-racial understanding; (b) critical thinking, cognitive skills, intellectual engagement and motivation, and intellectual self-confidence; (c) personal outcomes including self-confidence and identity formation; and (d) democratic citizenship learning outcomes such as civic engagement, leadership skills, and pluralistic orientation (see, for review). In addition, process outcomes reflect the ways that diversity has enriched students' experiences of diversity while in college and can be viewed as intermediate because they influence other types of outcomes such as satisfaction, retention, and persistence (Milem, 2003). Yet even if a clear causal link between the educational environment and diversity competence is found, the processes that underpin this causal relationship are far from clear (Sidanius, Levin, van Laar, & Sears, 2008).

The research literature substantiates the thesis that diversity learning arises from cognitive dissonance or the disequilibrium that arises from encountering difference. Based on the theories of Jean Piaget (1975/1985) and others, experiences that are novel or different from one's current views can generate cognitive growth as individuals must reconcile the novel interaction with existing beliefs or change his/her views to accommodate the new information (Bowman, 2010a; Bowman & Brandenberger, 2012; Denson & Chang, 2015; Gurin et al., 2002; Gurin, Nagda, & Lopez, 2004).

The broad racial framing of American society by white Americans has taken shape in racial stereotypes (an aspect of belief), racial narratives, and interpretations that integrate cognitive aspects of understanding, racialized emotions, racial images and language aspects, and inclinations to discriminatory action (Feagin, 2013). College diversity experiences whether classroom based or through informal interactions operate through processes of enlightenment, such as by increasing awareness of the plight of others, or through contact such as structured interactions between majority and minority group members, or both (Dovidio, Gaertner, Stewart, Esses, ten Vergert, & Hodson, 2004). Enlightenment and contact can stimulate internal cognitive and emotional processes or mediators that translate these experiences into reductions in prejudice, discrimination and stereotyping (Dovidio et al., 2004). Empirical studies have demonstrated that campus diversity experiences can result in growth in cognitive skills of thinking and reasoning and cognitive tendencies in terms of an inclination toward certain styles or modes of thinking (Bowman, 2010a). For example, a meta-analysis from 17 studies with a total of 77,029 undergraduate students confirmed the relation of college diversity experiences to cognitive development, with the strongest relation arising from interpersonal interactions with racial diversity (Bowman, 2010a). Diversity coursework and workshops were also positively correlated with cognitive growth (Bowman, 2010a).

Consider how Paul, a white male who graduated from a Midwestern public research university and is now an entrepreneur, describes the cognitive growth that resulted from his informal interactions with diverse individuals on his campus:

it shouldn't come as any surprise that interactions with non-white individuals were a frequent occurrence—the campus is incredibly diverse. I suppose that the quality of my interactions improved as the years went by and I began to understand and comprehend how difficult it must be to come from a foreign country, attend a top notch university when English is your second language, not have any social support and struggle to understand cultural norms. I mean, it was hard for me and I was born and raised right here. I suppose my interactions and consciousness evolved from a state of not knowing/caring of others struggles as minorities to a state of really being humbled by just how easy I have it in relation to most other folks.

Yet the attainment of diversity learning outcomes can be hindered by the lack of an intentional and cohesive curricular and cocurricular approach to diversity. Take how Martin, the African-American clinical professor cited earlier, describes the "lackluster" approach of his university to incorporating cultural competence in the curriculum:

I always find it hysterical when universities and programs talk about the need for diversity and addressing culture competency within their curriculum and our program is so diverse and you look around and it isn't. And... you are saying, this doesn't reflect what you say you are. I have always been observant of words and actions. So if you said you would do one thing, I always expect it to occur, so in college... it would be a lackluster sort of approach. It did not sit well with me. And it still doesn't in academia. It doesn't sit well with me when departments or universities do that. That was my first real experience with it at the university I attended.

Beyond the benefits to the individual, democracy outcomes create a widening circle leading to the realization of economic and societal benefits (Milem, 2003). Viewed from the lens of society as a whole, cultural democracy is a critical component of a democratic society and a political democracy (Banks, 2008). In other words, a democratic society is the field in which cultural pluralism flourishes. The concept of cultural pluralism denotes a society that is multicultural and composed of different cultures that are respected and valued. In this context, the role of democratically accountable educational institutions with respect to different social and cultural groups is to be nonrepressive, deliberative, and nondiscriminatory and to recognize the cultural identities of those they represent (Gutmann, 1994b). This viewpoint counteracts hierarchical views of certain cultures as superior to others and of the dominant culture as taking precedence over other cultural perspectives.

Table 3 below highlights how the educational benefits realized by students on diverse campuses yield both economic and societal benefits.

TABLE 3
Educational Benefits of Diverse College and University Campuses

Type of Benefit

Economic/Private Sector Benefits	Societal Benefits
Cultivation of a workforce with greater levels of cross-cultural competence	Decreased occupational and residential segregation in society
Attraction of best available talent pool	Greater engagement with social and political issues
Enhanced marketing efforts	Decreased stereotyping and lower levels of ethnocentrism
Better problem-solving abilities	Higher levels of service to community/civic organizations
Greater organizational flexibility	Increased service by physicians of color to the most medically underserved communities
Affirmative action in employment leads to: - decreased job discrimination - decreased wage disparities - decreased occupational segregation - increased occupational aspirations for women and people of color - greater organizational productivity	Greater equity in society
	A more educated citizenry

Source: Milem, 2003.

In this context, the question arises as to how the attainment of democracy learning outcomes and, by extension, diversity competence, relate to the overall goals of a liberal education. This relationship has been the explicit focus of a number of initiatives undertaken by the Association of American Colleges and Universities (AAC&U) over the past decade (see, for example, AAC&U, 2007; Dey, Ott, Antonaros, Barnhardt, & Holsapple, 2010; Gaston, 2015).

The Relation of Liberal Education to Diversity Competence

The term "liberal education" was coined by the Romans and pertained to an approach to education of the Greeks that linked a broad education and liberty (Zakaria, 2015). In America today, however, the concept of a broad-based liberal education is out of favor and has few defenders (Zakaria, 2015). An emphasis on skills-based learning and vocationalism in an era of technology and globalization has taken root, whereas an open-ended exploration of knowledge is seen as a "road to nowhere" (Zakaria, 2015, p. 16). Furthermore, although liberal education is most frequently associated with liberal arts colleges, only about 1.8% of undergraduates attend these institutions, whereas 52% of American undergraduates are enrolled in 2-year or even less than 2-year institutions (Zakaria, 2015).

Although descriptions of liberal education are often amorphous, two basic schools of thought have arisen historically in its conceptualization: the fluid model and the core model (Menand, 1997). The fluid model sees departmentalized fields as the intellectual DNA or sea in which the disciplines swim, transcending data or technique and yielding a set of intellectual skills rather than discrete bits of information (Menand, 1997). The operationalization of the fluid model in undergraduate education is the distribution requirement based on "a baptismal theory of knowledge" (Menand, 1997, p. 3). By contrast, the core model focuses on a set of core courses offered independently of academic departments that provide exposure to a discrete body of knowledge and specific works (Menand, 1997). The belief in a common core of knowledge that each educated person should possess is an essentialist approach based on the theory of general education (Howard, 1992; Menand, 1997).

In the fluid model tradition, Kimball (1997) argued two decades ago that a new metarationale, namely pragmatism, has begun to converge with liberal education, and that consensus has emerged around seven components of such education. These components include the need for a liberal education to be multicultural, elevate integration and general education rather than specialization, and promote citizenship (Kimball, 1997). In this sense, the educational process is seen as a source of integrative knowledge that helps students be lifelong learners and leaders who can work within diverse teams, balance the needs of others, and recognize the strengths and limits of their own and other perspectives (Reynolds-Keefer et al., 2011). Pragmatism, however, transcends individual economic and employer benefits, and invokes the notion of strengthening society and democracy (Astin, 1997).

Nonetheless, the typical college curriculum and cocurriculum shows little evidence of a core commitment to the preparation for responsible citizenship (Astin, 1997). The typical undergraduate rarely addresses equity questions, differential resources, power, and systemic advantage as part of the formal curriculum (Knefelkamp & Schneider, 1997).

Building on the fluid model and the pragmatist strain described earlier, the AAC&U has taken a leadership role in articulating the goals of a liberal education in terms of the comprehensive aims and outcomes essential for democratic citizenship and the development of individual talent (AAC&U, 2007). Such an educational approach views perspective taking as one of the foundational differences between narrow training and a horizon-expanding education (Schneider, 2010). In essence, perspective taking involves engaging "difficult difference" respectfully in considering alternative views that depart from an individual's own expected patterns, beliefs, and "grounded positions" (Schneider, 2010, p. ix). Yet only a third of students and professionals surveyed on 23 college campuses with 24,000 student and 9,000 administrators and faculty participating strongly agreed that their institutions have made perspective taking a major focus (Dey et al., 2010). Allied with the need for perspective taking, how can colleges and universities strengthen the connection between democracy learning outcomes and the development of diversity competence? We explore this question in the next section.

Common Ground: Democracy Learning Outcomes and Diversity Competence

Diversity competence and democracy learning outcomes are necessarily intertwined and share common ground. Yet the congeniality of diversity and democracy may not be self-evident, especially in light of potential tension between the cultural dimensions of citizenship and the unity needed for democracy (Gurin et al., 2004). In spite of these concerns, three powerful educational spheres of inquiry focused on social justice issues, offer the opportunity for common conceptual frameworks, complementary pedagogies, and allied learning outcomes: (a) diversity; (b) global learning; and (c) civic engagement (Musil, 2009). These intersecting spheres encompass a learning trajectory that moves from the self to others, culminating in cooperative work to achieve the public good (Musil, 2009). Five critical questions for students summarize the course of this progressive learning continuum (Musil, 2009, p. 57):

Who am I? (knowledge of self)

Who are we? (communal/collective knowledge)

What does it feel like to be them? (empathetic knowledge)

How do we talk with one another? (intercultural process knowledge)

How do we improve our shared lives? (applied, engaged knowledge)

A growing research literature on democracy outcomes as a distinct educational benefit of diversity identifies several types of outcomes, including civic engagement, leadership skills, and pluralistic orientation (see Chun & Evans, 2015, for a synopsis of these outcomes). Pluralistic orientation refers to the ability to see multiple perspectives, work cooperatively with diverse individuals, negotiate controversial issues, and maintain openness to challenges to one's own views (Engberg, 2007). In an expert report prepared for the 2003 Supreme Court cases of *Grutter v. Bollinger* (539 U.S. 306) and *Gratz v. Bollinger* (539 U.S. 244), Gurin also identified "racial/cultural engagement" and "compatibility of differences" as important democracy learning outcomes (Gurin, 1999). Racial/cultural engagement involves cultural knowledge and awareness as well as motivation to participate in activities that promote racial understanding. Compatibility of differences addresses the belief that basic values are common across racial and ethnic groups, recognizes the constructive aspects of group conflict, and posits the capacity to overcome divisiveness within society (Gurin, 1999).

A number of empirical and longitudinal studies have demonstrated the link between diversity-related educational experiences and democracy learning outcomes. For example, a meta-analytic study using 27 works with a total of 175,950 undergraduates found that college experiences of diversity that result in direct or "proximal" outcomes of increased cultural knowledge or awareness and empathy lead, in turn, to "distal" outcomes such as attitudes and behaviors not specifically related to diversity, including leadership skills, orientations toward social justice and pluralism, and civic action (Bowman, 2011). The study found a positive relationship between diversity and civic engagement that included civic attitudes, skills, and behavioral interactions (Bowman, 2011). Preliminary analysis of key works also found that relationships between diversity experiences and civic outcomes were quite similar for both minority and white students (Bowman, 2011). Although gains in civic engagement were realized regardless of the type of diversity experience such as curricular or cocurricular diversity, the greatest gains derived from interpersonal interactions with racial diversity (Bowman, 2011).

Other representative studies include a longitudinal field study of 87 participants in the Intergroup Relations Program (IGR) at the University of Michigan, a curricular program for first-year students that addresses conditions that make diversity and democracy compatible, and a longitudinal survey of 1,670 students (Gurin et al., 2004). The results confirmed the relation of diversity experiences with increased perspective-taking and more frequently expressed democratic sentiments such as greater mutuality in learning about their own and other groups, enhanced commonality in values relating to work and family from other groups, as well as increased commitment to community involvement (Gurin et al., 2004).

Similarly, a substantive research study using four national databases that includes three longitudinal datasets conclusively links diversity and civic-minded practices with student outcomes (Hurtado & DeAngelo, 2012). Results of the study indicate that in the first year, the peer environment and informal interactions with diverse students that involved meaningful discussions of race and ethnicity are associated with changes in student habits of mind for learning (Hurtado & DeAngelo, 2012). Additional factors in changing student mindsets are the amount and quality of faculty contact, as well as participation in faculty research projects (Hurtado & DeAngelo, 2012). Gains in students' pluralistic orientation and preparation for a diverse workplace were associated with repeated exposure to diverse opinions, values, and cultures, as well as exposure to real-world problems (Hurtado & DeAngelo, 2012). An important finding of the study is that timing is a critical consideration in advancing students' diversity skills, since freshmen often decline in terms of pluralistic orientation during the first year of college (Hurtado & DeAngelo, 2012). The sooner students can become engaged in activities that engage their interest, skills, and confidence; the more likely they will be to seek opportunities to build upon civic-related and diversity learning (Hurtado & DeAngelo, 2012). Similarly, a longitudinal study of 1,865 students in 17 colleges and universities found that diversity experiences during the first year of college led to an increase in others types of diversity experiences in the senior year (Bowman, 2012).

Yet the pace of advancing diversity competence may vary depending on a student's preparation and preexisting orientation. A first- and second-year longitudinal study of 4,697 students at nine different public institutions found that students entering college with a stronger orientation toward pluralism were more likely to select diversity experiences that strengthen intergroup learning or mutual reciprocal learning about social identity and that reduce intergroup anxiety or the discomfort with individuals not in one's own racial group (Engberg, 2007). Further, students at institutions with higher levels of structural diversity were more likely to engage in positive cross-racial interactions, with a positive, indirect effect on pluralistic orientation in their second year (Engberg, 2007).

Consider the observations of Michael, a white male who graduated from a Midwestern public research university as an example of the impact of diversity on pluralistic orientation and preparation for a diverse workplace. Michael is now employed as a technical recruiter in information technology. His undergraduate experiences and specifically a powerful cross-cultural psychology course affected his subsequent ability to understand diverse perspectives in the workplace:

I developed or at least strengthened the ability to be non-ethnocentric. These classes helped me view others' perspectives and apply it to real conversations and working relationships with people from varying backgrounds, ethnicities, and/or races. I think it is extremely important for the workplace now, the industry that I am in. When I am speaking with people who have relocated to the United States to seek a career in IT, it's important for me to identify what's important to these individuals, how can I best communicate with them. And also with my colleagues at work—a lot of them came from similar backgrounds—I think it's also being able to communicate with them from an outsider's perspective, "Ok, this is kind of what this person is thinking," and I need to be able to explain that in the best way possible in a work setting. . . . I think if I hadn't taken that approach and if I don't think about diversity and how it affects my office or my day-to-day work, I think we would be as successful as we are.

In light of the common ground that connects diversity competence and democracy outcomes, we next explore ways in which curricular practices in higher education are being redesigned to accomplish these objectives.

Cross-Cutting Educational Approaches to Democracy Outcomes

As we have noted, the AAC&U has assumed a national leadership role in the effort to make liberal education more inclusive and engaged with global, social, ethical, economic, and civic issues (Schneider, 2015). In particular, the General Education Maps and Markers initiative launched by the AAC&U, offers a coherent approach to general education that, among other objectives, will allow students to attain greater awareness of their culture and of others, and to develop the capacity to pursue career advancement, active citizenship, and global engagement (Gaston, 2015).

Despite the critical link between diversity and democracy outcomes, the development of a coherent and intentional approach to diversity learning in the undergraduate experience remains an elusive goal for many colleges and universities. For the most part, institutions have adopted a "helter-skelter" approach to democracy outcomes and civic engagement, without embedding civic learning at the academic core (Musil, 2003, p. 4). The Civic Learning Spiral developed by a working group convened by the AAC&U for their 5-year initiative, Greater Expectations: Goals for Learning as a Nation Goes to College, graphically portrays the civic learning continuum (Musil, 2009). Beginning with the self that is situated in a social location and historical context, the components of the spiral include the interconnected elements or braids of communities and cultures, values, skills, knowledge, and public action or practice (Musil, 2009, 2011). These aspects of civic learning are intertwined at each full turn as students synthesize civic learning through a wide range of curricular and co-curricular experiences during the course of their education (Musil, 2009).

The kinds of learning generated by civic engagement can be characterized in a progression of six phases that culminate in intercultural or multicultural understanding and the ability to navigate cultural boundaries as follows: (Musil, 2003).

- Exclusionary—civic disengagement characterized by a monocultural, gated academic environment with traditional curricular borders
- Oblivious—"drive-by" service learning that views the world with civic detachment
- Naïve—civic amnesia that overlooks power dynamics and legacies of exclusion
- Charitable—civic altruism that focuses on community service rather than empowerment
- Reciprocal—civic engagement that strengthens students' intercultural competencies and multicultural knowledge through reciprocal empowerment

- Generative—civic prosperity that enables students to navigate cultural borders and grasp the arts of democracy through systems, interpersonal processes, values, and political mechanisms.

The link between diversity learning outcomes and students' subsequent work and citizenship experiences is particularly salient in the framework proposed by the AAC&U with the acronym "LEAP"—"Liberal Education and America's Promise: Excellence for Everyone as a Nation Goes to College" (AAC&U, 2007). The LEAP initiative represents a bold reformatting of the aims of a liberal education. Launched in 2005 as a decade-long initiative, the LEAP Campus Action Network already includes 340 institutions committed to liberal education for all students, including historically underserved student populations (AAC&U, n.d.-a). In particular, LEAP shines a light on goals that strengthen global understanding, cultural competence, integrative learning, and civic engagement. Noting that democracies are established based on a "distinctive web of values" consisting of justice, equality, human dignity, responsibility, and freedom, a report from LEAP's leadership council indicates that most students never study these issues in a formal way and do not consider civic engagement a goal of college studies (AAC&U, 2007).

The four areas of essential learning outcomes identified by LEAP sharpen the focus on cultural competence: (a) knowledge of human cultures and the physical and natural world; (b) intellectual and practical skills; (c) personal and social responsibility; and (d) integrative learning. The learning outcome of personal and social responsibility explicitly identifies civic engagement and knowledge, both local and global, as well as intercultural knowledge and competence (AAC&U, 2007). These outcomes are expected to be solidified through active involvement with diverse communities and real-world issues. Seven principles of excellence characterize the LEAP framework, all of which have implications for the attainment of diversity competence (AAC&U, 2007):

- Aim High—And Make Excellence Inclusive
- Give Students a Compass
- Teach the Arts of Inquiry and Innovation

- Engage the Big Questions
- Connect Knowledge with Choices and Action
- Foster Civil, Intercultural, and Ethical Learning
- Assess Students' Ability to Apply Learning to Complex Problems

The LEAP VALUE Rubrics provide common tools for operationalizing and assessing student learning outcomes that were developed between 2007 to 2009 by teams of faculty and educators from over 100 institutions (AAC&U, n.d.-b). Three of the 16 common rubrics have direct applicability to this study: Intercultural Knowledge and Competence, Global Learning, and Civic Engagement.

The rubric for Intercultural Knowledge and Competence identifies cognitive, affective, and behavioral skills and characteristics that lead to effective interaction in differing cultural contexts (AAC&U, n.d.-b). This rubric charts a pathway to three distinctive outcomes: the meaningful engagement of others, placement of social justice in a historical and political context, and putting culture at the center of transformative learning (AAC& U, n.d.-b). The rubric on Global Learning emphasizes the construct of cultural diversity and addresses the need for a deep understanding of differing worldviews and power structures (AAC& U, n.d.-b). Ultimately, the LEAP framework is about making connections with the workplace and society as a whole.

A leading-edge example of how cultural competence can be translated into learning objectives is the rubric developed by the University of Maryland (UMD) as part of a general education requirement (UMD, 2015). Undergraduates must take either two courses in understanding plural societies or one such course coupled with a cultural competence course. The process of developing the UMD cultural competence rubric involved a faculty board that clarified the cultural competence learning outcomes with a focus on the skills needed to negotiate cross-cultural interactions both inside of and outside the classroom. The rubric was then reviewed by focus groups and through faculty surveys and finalized by a team of campus stakeholders. Forging the link with the accreditation process, the general education rubrics are expected to aid in the upcoming review by the Middle States Commission on Higher Education (Mont, Shorter-Gooden, Stevens, & Nash, 2015).

The cultural competence rubric draws on negotiation models and presumes that cultural competence is primarily a skill, which requires cognitive understanding and a need to change one's mindset to achieve integrative understanding (C. K. Stevens, personal communication, June 1, 2015). By identifying components of effective negotiation skills, the performance levels were written to reflect advancement of student skills in awareness, communication, and negotiation (UMD, n.d.).

Concluding Observations

In this chapter, we have explored the vital intersection between democracy learning outcomes and students' attainment of the diversity competence needed to function in a global society. Democracy learning outcomes have concrete economic and social benefits that expand students' horizons beyond their individual campuses and affect their future orientation toward citizenship.

Students' lives today are characterized by disruption rather than by certainty and by interdependence instead of insularity (AAC&U, 2007). Because studies indicate that Americans change jobs 10 times during the two decades after they turn 18, the AAC&U finds that employers and educators are beginning to reach consensus about the learning outcomes students need from college (AAC&U, 2007). The leading-edge work of the AAC&U offers pathways to outcomes that prepare students for careers in an interdependent, global society: civic engagement, diversity competence, and global learning. The retooling of general education requirements allows undergraduates to reach a diversity threshold in terms of awareness, skillsets, and actions.

Serious questions remain, however, regarding the extent to which most institutions of higher education have made headway in overcoming a "helter-skelter" approach to diversity competence and democracy learning outcomes (Musil, 2003). By contrast, the LEAP VALUE rubrics create a solid foundation for the development of approaches to diversity competence. In addition, the University of Maryland's rubric for intercultural competence is a powerful illustration of the collaborative work of faculty, administrators, and campus stakeholders in defining and assessing cultural competency learning outcomes as part of the general education curriculum.

If Musil's (2003) civic learning continuum resulting in student attainment of multicultural understanding is to take shape on a campus, concerted faculty and administrative action will be needed to reframe existing exclusionary, oblivious, and sometimes naïve approaches and advance progressively to the reciprocal and generative phases. Given the importance of diversity competence to democracy learning outcomes, in the next chapter, we present an overview of the ways diversity competence can be addressed in curricular, service learning, and co-curricular practices in the undergraduate experience.

Mapping the Educational Terrain
for Diversity Competence

I think that our university has tried and in some ways has succeeded
in that our general education requirements require a diversity core.
That kind of transactional piece is there and does exist. But it is
unfortunately very transactional in the way that they go through it.
A lot of students look at the diversity core as something that they can
check off and be done with. And students aren't really transformed
by it.

Tracey, a white student affairs professional and graduate
of a Western public research university

RECALL TRACEY'S OBSERVATIONS earlier in the monograph regarding the unwelcoming climate for minorities at her isolated, predominantly white Western research university. Her insights underscore the need to move beyond a transactional, check-box approach to diversity in undergraduate curricular requirements to a transformative educational experience. As a result, in this chapter, we explore key components of the curricular and cocurricular terrain for the attainment of diversity competence with a synthesis of illustrative best practices in these areas. As part of this discussion, we highlight strategic approaches that accelerate the capacity of campuses to realize diversity competency within the campus ecosystem including the recent introduction of diversity mapping assessment methodology and the integrative potential of regional accreditation processes coupled with the development of the Degree Qualifications Profile under the auspices of the Lumina Foundation.

To begin our brief survey of the campus topography for diversity, we share a visual process of mapping that has emerged as a means of graphically representing areas of strength and opportunity for growth in diversity engagement.

A Visual Methodology

In order to portray the integration of diversity work on a college campus, diversity mapping has emerged as a new methodology for conceptualizing how diversity is actualized both structurally and thematically (Halualani, Haiker, & Lancaster, 2010). This holistic process serves as a method of inquiry and provides a metric by which campuses can evaluate engagement with diversity (Halualani et al., 2010; Hurtado & Halualani, 2014). Already implemented at more than 20 universities, the diversity-mapping framework aligns and evaluates information regarding the organizational dimensions of diversity including curriculum, student learning objectives, budget allocations, and policies in an integrated framework designed to measure and achieve progress (Hurtado & Halualani, 2014). The evaluation includes an extensive curricular inventory in terms of course types, content, and general education requirements related to diversity (Halualani, Haiker, Lancaster, & Morrison, 2015). In addition, a key element of the mapping process involves analysis of the endurance and sustainability of diversity efforts, with a recommended strategic framework of 5 years (Halualani et al., 2015).

Of particular relevance to the evolution of cultural competency is a progressive Diversity Engagement and Learning Taxonomy Assessment (DELTA) that gauges the campus level of engagement with diversity by analyzing diversity initiatives, curricula, and programs across all divisions and units (Hurtado & Halualani, 2014). The mapping process involves a high reliance on data collection from all institutional divisions as well as electronic data analysis using SPSS and a qualitative coding software. Data are recorded in a spreadsheet that tracks specific components of diversity programs and course offerings (Halualani et al., 2015). This analysis yields a map that reflects lower to higher levels of campus engagement with diversity as follows (Halualani et al., 2015):

Level 1—Knowledge/awareness of diversity
Level 2—Skills including the application of intercultural competence
Level 3—Interaction with emphasis on intercultural interaction
Level 4—Advanced analysis including perspective taking
Level 5—Evaluation-critique involving critique of power differences
Level 6—Social agency and action
Level 7—Problem solving that involves multiple perspectives from all cultures/contexts

Grounded in an understanding of power differentials and the influence of normative cultural practices on campus climate, diversity mapping analyzes and critiques existing practices and identifies progressive attainment of intercultural or diversity competence. In essence, it supports a continuous process of organizational learning. This methodological assessment method provides both an evaluative and aspirational view of a campus' diversity efforts. As we shall see in the next section, progress in curricular change is evolutionary and often contested.

Campus Curricular Inventory for Diversity

Over the last several decades, higher education has undergone dramatic reform of the general education curriculum, most notably with the incorporation of multiculturalism (Nelson Laird & Engberg, 2011). Such efforts have often, however, been accompanied by contentious campus debates with success varying across institutions and a lack of uniformity in programmatic outcomes (Chang, 2002).

As a case in point, consider the long-standing battle over the incorporation of a diversity requirement in the undergraduate curriculum at the

University of California at Los Angeles (UCLA), one of the nation's most diverse top research universities. Faculty in the College of Arts and Sciences, the main undergraduate college, voted on the requirement in 2004 and 2012 and finally passed it by a narrow margin in 2014 (Jaschik, 2015). Not satisfied with this result, opponents filed a petition that forced a vote of the entire faculty, resulting in a vote of 916 to 487 in April 2015 (Jaschik, 2015). Arguments against the measure summarized by the Faculty Senate include the possibility that many students would take a course aligned with their own identity leading to a "ghettoization" effect and that no controlled studies have found a causal effect of diversity curriculum and self-reported student attitudes (Garrett, n.d.). Speaking against the requirement, UCLA political science professor Thomas Schwartz indicated, "Diversity is code for a certain set of politically correct or left leaning attitudes on college campuses. There's enough of that here" (Frank, 2014). He added, "I don't think students should be required to take an ideologically slanted or a politically slanted course" (Frank, 2014).

The recalcitrance to include even a minimal diversity requirement exemplifies the insistence on a color-blind society without the need to understand the plurality of perspectives and social identities present. Resistance to inclusion of diversity in the curriculum suggests a central, less visible but deep aspect of white racial framing that reinforces the preeminence of white virtue, intelligence, and superiority (Yancy & Feagin, 2015). The objection raised by the UCLA Faculty Senate indicating that controlled studies have not found a causal relationship between diversity courses and self-reported student attitudes overlooks the findings of both longitudinal and controlled empirical studies that have demonstrated the effects of diversity (see Bowman, 2009, 2010a, 2010b; Denson & Chang, 2009; Gurin, Nagda, & Zúñiga, 2013; Nelson Laird, 2005).

For example, a meta-analysis of 16 quantitatively based empirical studies found that diversity-related curricular and co-curricular activities that expanded individuals' content-based knowledge of other groups have a moderate effect on reducing racial bias (Denson, 2009). This study also found that white students tend to benefit more from these diversity-related interventions than minority students (Denson, 2009). Confirming these findings, a longitudinal study of 3,081 first-year students from 19 colleges and universities reported that white students receive greater benefits than minority students of color from taking a single diversity course (versus no courses) in terms of three variables: comfort with differences, relativistic appreciation of similarities and differences, and diversity of contact in diverse social and cultural interactions (Bowman, 2010b). Students who take two diversity courses had greater gains in diversity of contact than those who took only one and taking three or more courses increased the gains on all three variables (Bowman, 2010b). The results suggest that the curricular benefits of diversity are amplified when students take multiple diversity courses (Bowman, 2010b).

In another example, a study of 289 University of Michigan students found that students with greater experiences of diversity, particularly through enrollment in diversity coursework and positive diversity interactions, were more likely to score higher on academic self-confidence (Nelson Laird, 2005). In addition, students with more experiences with diversity were more likely to score higher on social agency in terms of a disposition to take action to improve society and correct injustice; and critical thinking (Nelson Laird, 2005). These research findings coupled with our interviews of recent college graduates suggest that the requirement for a single diversity course, which has become more widespread among colleges and universities, may not capitalize upon the needed educational benefits of diversity. By contrast, institutions such as the University of Massachusetts Amherst, Northern Arizona University, the University of Nebraska, the University of Maryland, and the University of Vermont have adopted a two-course or six-credit diversity-related requirement as part of the general education curriculum in order to deepen and broaden students' understanding of diversity.

Reinforcing the need for a more broad-based diversity curricular requirement, take the experiences of Marjorie, a white female at a predominantly white Midwestern public undergraduate college:

I know that we had one requirement for the bachelor's that we were supposed to take a diversity course; we could take a Chicano course, or Latino/Latina or African-American studies..., I feel that they should have an extra requirement for that would cover every single

issue 'cause some people would just take African-American stud-
ies 101; but in that course you are not learning about all aspects
of diversity that exist as well as everything that people should be
thinking about and so that we could do a better job at kind of
fixing the issues that we have.

Now working as a research assistant on a National Institutes of Health grant dealing with gender and race biases, Marjorie does not recall learning anything about workplace barriers to diversity as an undergraduate. As she explains,

I don't know if as an undergrad we really talked about it a lot? I
can't think of anything that we really discussed in any of my courses
or my positions. I know the job I have now I am learning more and
more about diversity within the workplace. . . .

Although diversity is addressed in required general education require-ments, it also is the subject of departmental and disciplinary offerings and ma-jors such as women's or ethnic studies, and communicated through pedagog-ical strategies such as intergroup dialogue (Nelson Laird & Engberg, 2011). Social justice education represents a major curricular focus that addresses the full, democratic participation of all groups in society, emphasizes social agency and responsibility, and the equitable distribution of power and resources (Bell, 2016). As such, it addresses the interlocking features of oppression such as manifested in racism, sexism, heterosexism, classism, ableism, ageism, reli-gious oppression, and transgender oppression (Bell, 2016). It provides a sub-stantive analysis of how these features are woven together to affect life op-portunities and reinforce inequality within the individual, interpersonal, and institutional domains (Bell, 2016).

Few studies, however, have examined pedagogical approaches across the spectrum of required and elective diversity courses in terms of specific course elements and degree of diversity inclusivity (Nelson Laird & Engberg, 2011). Rather than focusing simply on course content or course description, Nelson Laird's (2011, 2014) model of diversity inclusivity provides nine elements that are important to diversity courses on a continuum from not at all inclusive to highly inclusive. These elements include the purpose and goals of the course, its content, foundations, the pedagogy, the ability to adjust to the diverse needs of students, methods of assessment and evaluation, as well as the approach of the instructor and the approach to learners.

An alternative way of conceptualizing diversity inclusivity in the curriculum is the concept of multicultural course transformation. Multicultural course change represents the effort to modify a given course to include multicultural perspectives and strategies (Kitano, 1997; Stanley, Saunders, & Hart, 2005). The process of multicultural course transformation is seen as a continuum that addresses four key dimensions: content, instructional strategies, assessment of student knowledge, and classroom approaches (Decker Lardner, 2003; Kitano, 1997). This continuum is modeled after Banks' (1993) model of multicultural curriculum transformation in the K–12 setting (Banks, 1993; Melnick, 2000; Stanley et al., 2005). In this evolutionary framework, exclusive courses center on mainstream experiences and perspectives of the discipline, whereas inclusive courses present alternative perspectives through an additive approach that does not alter curricular structures. At the highest level, a transformative approach conceptualizes the goals, structure, and nature of the curriculum to include the perspectives of diverse groups, and the social/action approach that engages students as agents for social change (Banks, 1993; Kitano, 1997; Melnick, 2000; Stanley et al., 2005).

Take the commentary of David, a white male graduate with a major in biology, who describes the transformative, multicultural perspective offered in a biology course he took at a Midwestern public comprehensive university. David describes the impact of the course on understanding the *umwelt* or the biological grounding that underpins different cultural experiences of the world and the environment:

> *The core grounding that helped shape who I am and how I think were the courses that forced me think outside of my normal focus. For example, the class with the strongest emphasis of how I think today was a course that took a biological vantage point in seeing and understanding topics such as history, art, food, culture, religion, medicine. This allowed to apply scientific principles to*

understand how things are today. For example, there is a biological reason behind the prohibition of consumption of pork for Islamic culture and cattle in India. There are innumerable examples of scientific principles to explain our world and umwelt.

With the need for diversity inclusivity in mind, we now explore the ways in which campuses have initiated curricular change and the key attributes of successful practices.

Features of Curricular Best Practices

In analyzing the implementation of curricular approaches to diversity and cultural competence, salient characteristics of successful transformational initiatives include the following elements: (a) active, mission-driven leadership at all institutional levels emanating from the board of trustees, president, and provost and including deans and department chairs; (b) deliberative, planned, and sustained efforts that address student learning outcomes for citizenship and work in a diverse global society; (c) faculty buy-in, particularly through faculty senate action and by building initial support in larger colleges of an institution such as the college of liberal arts; (d) faculty-led committees that work collaboratively in disciplinary areas; (e) an effective assessment process of the current and desired states; (f) connection to external stakeholders including the community, alumni, and employers as part of workforce development; and (g) a supportive infrastructure such as through faculty teaching and learning centers to provide tools and resources for curricular transformation. The spectrum of change processes is highly varied and necessarily connected with institutional context and mission. Processes range from more nascent initiatives at some institutions to systemic change that has been sustained over an extended time period. Even at institutions like Pennsylvania State University, which has been in the vanguard of diversity change with a strategic 5-year planning cycle, the development of a curriculum with intercultural and internal competencies remains in its early phases. An evaluation conducted by Halualani and associates conducted in 2013 at Penn State using the DELTA mapping methodology concluded that evidence suggested that diversity-related courses were at level 1 in terms of knowledge awareness and there was a lack of systemic evidence of attainment of higher levels (Halualani, Haiker, & Thi, 2013).

With these characteristics in mind, a prominent example of multicultural curricular transformation is the initiative undertaken at Northern Illinois University (NIU) that began in 1994. Led by the executive vice president and provost and the Committee on Multicultural Curriculum Transformation (CMCT), this university-wide effort resulted in transformation of most of the curriculum in certain disciplines and of specific courses in others (Krishnamurthi, 2005). The goals of the initiative were not only to effect comprehensive multicultural curricular transformation but also to promote inclusive classroom environments and create a model for institution-wide transformation (Krishnamurthi, 2005).

In tandem with this initiative, a Multicultural Course Transformation Institute was formed that served over 200 faculty between 1994 and 2013 and provided insight into the cultural contexts students come from as well as the perspectives that diverse students bring to the classroom (J. Hamlet, personal communication, February 12, 2016). The infrastructure supporting this comprehensive effort included the Faculty Development and Instructional Design Center, campus units focused on resources for particular groups, policies, committees, commissions, and task forces (Krishnamurthi, 2005). A comprehensive website provides a wealth of resources on multicultural curriculum transformation (Northern Illinois University, 2015).

In 2015, NIU took additional steps by reorienting the general education curriculum with a more explicit focus on cultural competence and global learning through the Progressive Learning in Undergraduate Studies (PLUS) initiative. This initiative sought to address the "menu-driven sprawl" of the previous general education program viewed by students as pointless and disconnected and replace it with three broad knowledge domains: Creativity and Critical Analysis, Nature and Technology, and Society and Culture (AAC&U, 2015). Among the eight baccalaureate and general education outcomes identified by the PLUS taskforce are intercultural competence and integrating knowledge of global connections and interdependencies (AAC&U, 2015).

Although the new General Education PLUS initiative has received widespread buy-in across NIU's colleges, its newness precludes assessment of its effectiveness at this time (J. Hamlet, personal communication, February 12, 2016).

One of the significant developments at NIU has been the recognition that although a multicultural curriculum is important, cultural competency in faculty's pedagogical practices is also a priority (J. Hamlet personal communication, February 12, 2016). Faculty and staff training on cultural competence is in the planning stages. With the hiring of its first chief diversity officer in 2015, the university has focused on bringing students, faculty, staff, and students together on initiatives such as the Diversity Dialogues program that addresses difficult and often controversial diversity issues.

Elements of the successful change process at NIU include high-level support from the executive vice president and provost, creation of a faculty and staff committee chaired by the associate vice president for academic diversity and chief diversity officer to be charged with assessing future diversity initiatives, recognition of the need for buy-in across the colleges, and development of the needed supportive infrastructure.

In another example, the first goal of the 2012–2020 strategic plan of the University of Colorado at Colorado Springs (n.d.) is to "foster academic programs that service diverse communities and develop intellectually curious graduates who are globally and culturally competent." As an example of curricular change, the Ethnic Studies and Women's Studies Programs have joined forces in a single department to create a major and minor that are intersectional in approach with courses focused on the relationship between privilege and oppression that are both local and global (A. Herrera, personal communication, September 21, 2015). The department pioneered an annual curriculum transformation workshop called the Knapsack Institute that addresses not only forms of discrimination based on oppression but also critical whiteness studies and research on masculinities (Ferber & Herrera, 2005). The goal of the institute is to assist faculty in generating course subject matter and to develop classroom strategies to deal with the diversity of experience that students bring to that setting (Ferber & Herrera, 2005). The development of assessment measures to evaluate this curricular change is underway.

In a third example, at the University of Missouri at Columbia, following student demonstrations and protests related to diversity and inclusion in fall 2015, a proposal for a diversity requirement in the undergraduate curriculum is under discussion (University of Missouri, 2015). Following over a year of meetings and discussions with students, faculty, and staff, the Faculty Council Diversity Enhancement Committee has proposed a pilot study to determine the effectiveness of this approach in applying cultural competency in the curriculum (University of Missouri). Of particular note is the leadership by the Faculty Senate and its effort to include all stakeholders as well as assess the efficacy of a diversity requirement in terms of student learning outcomes.

Given these examples, we next examine service learning and its potentially substantive role in attaining diversity outcomes within the context of academic courses. Because service learning is often viewed as a cocurricular program, we address its impact when incorporated as an integral part of curricular content.

Service Learning as a Bridge to Diversity Competence

Academic service learning occupies a unique niche in the academy and, as such, can form a natural bridge to enhancing diversity competence. It is a form of experiential education that provides an avenue for students, faculty, and the university to engage with the community (Ward, 2003). Service learning is amenable to a cultural perspective as a way of repairing social networks, fostering respect for diversity, and encouraging volunteerism and civic engagement (Butin, 2010). An emerging body of literature advocates for multicultural service learning as a means to challenge inequality and build community (Boyle-Baise, 2002; Pasquesi, 2013).

Yet the thinking in higher education has been that service learning is outside the classroom, on a student's own time (Vogelgesang & Astin, 2000). Far too often, service learning has been positioned as a cocurricular practice, viewed by some faculty as a time-consuming and atheoretical pedagogy that detracts from progress toward tenure attainment (Butin, 2006). In fact, course-based service needs to be distinguished from cocurricular community service (Vogelgesang & Astin, 2000). Course-based service learning uses reflection including discussions, journals, and papers to connect the service experience to course material (Astin, Vogelgesang, Ikeda, & Yee, 2000).

Institutions can have variable approaches to service learning based on mission, geographical location, student demographics, and history (Ward, 2003). The literature indicates, however, that the predominantly white institutions have emphasized service centered on the campus and doing for the community, whereas special-focus colleges and universities (SFCUs) (tribal colleges, Hispanic-serving institutions, and historically black institutions) have integrated service into their mission through a focus on doing with the community (Ward & Wolf-Wendel, 2000). Simply viewing service learning in terms of helping or deficit models diminishes the reciprocal power that can be attained between students and the community (Weah, Simmons, & Hall, 2000).

A longitudinal study of 22,236 students using data that compared the outcomes of service learning and cocurricular community service found that 29.9% had participated in course-based community service, 46.5% had participated in other forms of community service, and 23.6% did not participate in any community service during college (Vogelgesang & Astin, 2000). The study demonstrated that the values of "commitment to promoting racial understanding" and "commitment to activism" were significantly affected by course-based service over generic community service (Vogelgesang & Astin, 2000, p. 30). In addition, it revealed that for all academic outcomes, such as critical thinking, writing skills, and grade point average, as well as for some affective ones, participating in course-based service learning had a positive effect that exceeded the effect of generic community service (Astin et al., 2000).

Consistent with the outward-facing focus in clinical or public-oriented professions, a positive correlation between service and community-based learning and cultural competence has been made in health-related fields, such as nursing, counseling, and community health, as well as physical education and agriculture-related fields through a limited number of empirical studies (see, for example, Amerson, 2010; Flannery & Ward, 1999; Housman, Meaney, Wilcox, & Cavazos, 2012; McKenna & Ward, 1996;

Meaney, Bohler, Kopf, Hernandez, & Scott, 2008; Smith et al., 2014; Ward, 1995). One study of 125 students involved in community-based learning found, for example, three major themes related to cultural competence: (a) greater "ethnic consciousness"; (b) enhanced personal and intellectual development related to cultural competence and health issues; and (c) empowerment of students as citizens contributing to the community (Flannery & Ward, 1999).

Ironically, however, service learning is most frequently used by the most marginalized and least powerful faculty (minorities, women, and untenured faculty) and by the most vocationally oriented and "softest" disciplines such as education and social work (Butin, 2006). In these disciplines, however, service learning often plays an integral part in professional training and is required by some accrediting bodies. At the same time, service learning suffers from serious pedagogical issues: it is premised on single, full-time nonindebted, childless students pursuing a liberal education; it focuses on "border-crossing identity categories" such as race, ethnicity, class, and disability which have already become occupied by an increasing percentage of students; and it may come to signify a luxury for the privileged few who represent the "Whitest of the White" (Butin, 2006, p. 482). Furthermore, inherent dilemmas can arise in service learning undertaken from a cultural perspective when these experiences reinforce students' deficit views of diverse others, such as when students volunteer in a homeless shelter and see the confirmation of their worst stereotypes through violent or sexist behavior (Butin, 2010).

An example of course-based service learning that connects with the community and is specifically designed to strengthen diversity competence, is Professor Phil Tajitsu Nash's Asian Pacific American (APA) Public Policy Course at the University of Maryland. This course requires students to conduct a 1-hour, videotaped oral history of an APA community leader, formulate a reflection memo on the experience, and make a formal presentation to the class (P. T. Nash, personal communication, June 3, 2015). Cultural competency activities such as visits to the Smithsonian and Chinatown are integrated in the course curriculum throughout the semester (P. T. Nash, personal communication, June 3, 2015). This course benefited the community by creating a library of oral histories of APA community members and by strengthening students' empathy and critical thinking through a reflective process and meta-processing of discussions (P. T. Nash, personal communication, February 10, 2016). In Nash's words, the project has created greater awareness among all involved that "cultural competence is essential to our survival as a species on this planet" (P.T. Nash, personal communication, February 10, 2016).

On a national level, the Campus Compact, a coalition of nearly 1,100 members, is the only educational association dedicated entirely to campus-based civic engagement and offers an array of resources in support of service learning (Campus Compact, 2015). These resources include an advanced service learning toolkit, service-learning syllabi, program models, and resource guidelines.

As with other efforts to address cultural competency, service-learning initiatives need to be carefully and intentionally planned with the desired learning outcomes in mind. Instead of deficit-based approaches to the community, course-based service learning needs to connect with diverse community groups in two-way interactions that strengthen reciprocity and mutual understanding.

Campus Cocurricular Inventory for Diversity

Cocurricular programs that build and reinforce diversity competence include study abroad programs, internships, leadership programs, residential living-learning communities, community service, and diversity-related campus events. Given the broad array of cocurricular practices and the limited research on their impact on diversity learning outcomes, we touch only on several areas that are associated with enhanced cultural competence, work across differences, and social justice. In particular, consistent with Allport's (1954) contact theory that under the appropriate conditions intergroup contact is one of the most effective means of reducing prejudice, campus programs that promote cross-racial contact have been associated with reductions in prejudice as well as with academic, cognitive, psychological, and civic outcomes not specifically related to diversity (Allport, 1979; Bowman, 2013b). We shall discuss Allport's theory further in the sixth chapter in terms of the optimal conditions for intergroup contact.

One of the most prominent cocurricular programs for promoting diversity competence is through study abroad programs. At the same time, as mentioned earlier in the monograph, institutions may not necessarily have considered how to ensure that student growth occurs in this area (Twombly et al., 2012), Further, study abroad programs focus rather exclusively on cultural differences that arise from differing nation states. Educators and policymakers need to guard against the "almost knee-jerk expectation" that international experience leads to cultural competence unless these programs are specifically designed to lead to student growth in this area (Twombly et al., 2012, p. 111).

At the same time, research finds that students who study abroad exhibit positive change in several aspects of intercultural competence on their return, including global perspective or world-mindedness and intercultural awareness or sensitivity (Twombly et al., 2012). Although this awareness pertains typically to differences among cultures in nation states, it is arguably transferable to the dimensions of diversity that transcend specific host cultures and strengthen diversity competence.

Residential living-learning communities represent a promising practice for enhancing diversity competence. Residential learning communities can be especially influential, as they tend to be associated with greater social interaction with peers and extracurricular involvement, higher persistence and graduation rates, and greater gains in critical thinking and reading comprehension (Zhao & Kuh, 2004). Although existing research on learning communities often is based on anecdotal evidence or program evaluations, a study of 80,479 freshman and seniors from 365 institutions drawn from the National Survey of Student Engagement (NSSE) found that all types of learning communities are linked positively with engaging in diversity-related activities (Zhao & Kuh, 2004).

An exemplary practice that combines curricular and co-curricular experiences related to diversity and cultural competence is the Social Justice Living Learning Community at Florida State University. This learning community accommodates approximately 30 students who live on the same floor, enroll in curricular work in social justice, and undertake cocurricular programs collectively such as community service (Guthrie, Jones, Osteen, & Hu, 2013). The community is specifically geared toward students who wish to engage in open and progressive conversations related to the dimensions of difference and identity (Florida State University, n.d.),

Because students may often not be aware of the ways in which their cocurricular experiences contribute to their diversity progress, San Diego State University (SDSU) offers a cocurricular transcript that provides an opportunity for students to track their own developmental growth as they progress through a number of diversity-related programs (Bruce, 2012). This transcript complements their academic transcript and strengthens ties with diverse members of the campus community (Bruce, 2012). In addition, the university created the first Cultural Competency Certificate Program in the California State University System designed to prepare graduates as leaders in a diverse workforce through a curriculum involving cultural diversity seminars, service learning, and a learning portfolio (SDSU, n.d.). The 1-year program has been recently redesigned and is focused on preparing students for future careers in diverse cultural settings (T. Starck, personal communication, February 21, 2016). As such, it explores many aspects of intercultural issues with a view to providing students with a greater understanding of power and privilege and an increased consciousness of social justice issues (T. Starck, personal communication, February 21, 2016).

Given this overview of curricular and cocurricular practices that strengthen diversity competence, we now explore how the processes of regional accreditation as well as the Degree Qualifications Profile developed under the auspices of the Lumina Foundation, can enhance integrated campus efforts to address the attainment of diversity competence.

Linking Diversity Competence to Accreditation Criteria

In addressing the development of diversity competence, the systems-based approach of regional accreditation processes offers the opportunity to address the interrelationships among the structural, physical, psychological, and learning dimensions of the campus ecosystem. The outcomes-based focus of accreditation review relies upon a culture of evidence that can be used to bolster, accelerate, and build accountability for diversity-related programs across multiple domains. Major diversity-related themes that emerge from accreditation criteria include the following:

Institutional integrity—Does the institution say what it values and then do what it values?

Structural diversity—Do faculty role models reflect the changing demographics of the nation and of student enrollment? Is the student body diverse?

Equitable processes—Does the institution have equitable processes related to hiring, evaluation, and promotion?

Student learning outcomes—Do student learning outcomes prepare students for participation in a global society and diverse democracy?

Among the most prominent examples are the guiding values and accreditation criteria of the Higher Learning Commission (HLC) that reference diversity and multiculturalism. The HLC governs postsecondary educational institutions in the North Central region of 19 states. One of the commission's 10 guiding values addresses "education for a diverse, technological, globally connected world" (HLC, 2015c). Specifically this value identifies the need for students to obtain the civic learning and enhanced intellectual capabilities needed for workforce success within the social context of a diverse, 21st century world (HLC, 2015c). Further, the accreditation criterion for institutional mission requires that the university or college understand the relationship between its mission and the diversity of society in two respects:

1. The institution addresses its role in a multicultural society.
2. The institution's processes and activities reflect attention to human diversity as appropriate within its mission and for the constituencies it serves (HLC, 2015a).

In its teaching and learning criterion, the HLC requires that "the education offered by the institution recognizes the human and cultural diversity of the world in which students live and work" (HLC, 2015a).

The HLC offers three pathways to accreditation: (a) a standard pathway; (b) an open pathway; and (c) the Academic Quality Improvement Program (AQIP). The open pathway developed beginning in 2009 and the AQIP pathway implemented in 1999 emphasize the integration of a campus ecosystem and quality improvement initiatives that support diversity-learning outcomes.

The Open Pathway requires an institution to undertake a major quality improvement initiative during years 5 and 9 of the 10-year review cycle (HLC, 2015d). Among the list of most common topics submitted as part of this requirement are cultural competency and developing a quality culture (HLC, 2015d). Beginning in 2009, demonstration projects were undertaken by the HLC to test the new Open Pathway model in collaboration with participating institutions. Between 2011 and 2013, the third test project by HLC in collaboration with 23 institutions was the pilot of a Degree Qualifications Profile (DQP) for associate's, baccalaureate, and master's degrees under the auspices of the Lumina Foundation (Rogers, Holloway, & Priddy, 2014).

The significance of the DQP for diversity competency lies in its emphasis on integrative learning as well as the identification of civic and global learning as one of the five categories of learning outcomes. The other four categories are (a) intellectual skills that include engaging diverse perspectives among other criteria; (b) applied and collaborative learning; (c) specialized knowledge; and (d) broad, integrative knowledge. The learning outcomes are intertwined and mutually reinforcing as illustrated in a spider web diagram that highlights the flexibility of approaches from different institutions in mission and areas of strength (Lumina Foundation, 2014). The DQP was "beta" tested at more than 400 colleges and universities in 45 states and serves as an important benchmark for the review and evaluation of general education requirements (Adelman, Ewell, Gaston, & Schneider, 2011; Lumina Foundation, 2014). The DQP is a prime example of the integral relationship between diversity learning outcomes and accreditation.

The AQIP pathway is HLC's other alternative accreditation pathway that emphasizes continuous improvement. AQIP involves a systems portfolio structure that integrates quality improvement initiatives in six major categories (Higher Learning Commission, 2015b).

- Helping Students Learn
- Meeting Student and Other Key Stakeholder Needs
- Valuing Employees
- Planning and Leading
- Knowledge Management and Resource Stewardship
- Quality Overview

The Quality Overview category emphasizes the culture and infrastructure of the institution and how all quality improvement initiatives are integrated and contribute to the improvement of the institution (Higher Learning Commission, 2015b). Both the Open Pathway and the AQIP process are value driven and process oriented, accenting the progress an institution is making toward its vision, mission, and goals.

In another example, the WASC Senior College and University Commission (WSCUC), which accredits senior colleges and universities in the western region emphasizes the importance of engaging students in an integrated course of study that will prepare them for citizenship, work, and lifelong learning and includes undergraduate programs that foster an appreciation for diversity, civic engagement, civic and ethical responsibility, and the ability to work with others (WSCUC, 2013). Similarly, the Middle States Commission on Higher Education, which covers institutions in the eastern region, emphasizes the need for undergraduate and general education programs to bring students into new areas of intellectual experience that include "expanding their cultural and global awareness and cultural sensitivity" (Middle States Commission on Higher Education, 2015, p. 7).

Concluding Observations

The development of an integrated curricular and cocurricular ecosystem for diversity remains a work in progress at most institutions. Inclusion of diversity requirements in the undergraduate curriculum remains a contested issue even at selective research universities. Many campuses have not gone beyond the requirement for a single diversity course often selected from a wide menu of choices. Take, for example, the comments of Tricia, a white, female, bisexual graduate of a predominantly white Midwestern public research university, who is now employed in a public charter school district working with English learners, lower socioeconomic communities, and undocumented students. As an undergraduate, Tricia was not aware that diversity was part of her university's mission and indicates the university could have made diversity part of required coursework for undergraduates, stating, "I had to go out of my way to take diversity courses."

Validating the findings of Hurtado and DeAngelo (2012) that timing is critical in the advancement of diversity skills, an elective on race and gender that Tricia took in her freshman year changed her mindset toward diversity: "It was the first semester of my freshman year and I had never been exposed to anyone ever talking about race and gender before; it was really eye opening for me." Furthermore, Tricia points out the absence of a university wide approach to diversity programming: "I know there were a lot of different types of diversity events that I could have attended but I never really heard about them. Maybe more [publicity for] schoolwide diversity events...the ones I heard about were smaller clubs."

When policymakers and educators fail to consider the extensive body of empirical evidence on the educational impact of diversity, this omission can lead to a serious deficit affecting the learning outcomes that students derive from a college education. As we have noted throughout this monograph, intentional, structural interventions are necessary to achieve diversity's benefits. In our student interviews, a repeated and common theme is the accidental and unplanned nature of diversity experiences that students encountered on their campuses. As Tracey explains,

> *And I think that the average student at my school if they were not that engaged, might not have had that same experience, unfortunately, because our campus still has work to do in terms of creating transformational experiences for students as it relates to diversity and inclusion. I think we are getting there and a priority in terms of what we are saying and our actions still need to catch up in certain places.*

Examples of best practices at universities such as at the University of Maryland and Northern Illinois University show how these institutions have undertaken significant changes to undergraduate programs to build an integrated approach to diversity learning outcomes in the curriculum and cocurriculum. The collaborative work of faculty and administration at these institutions models a progressive approach to strengthening multicultural course content and experiential approaches to student diversity competence.

In the next chapter, we turn to a discussion of identity development and structured intergroup interactions as a more specific illustration of how campus practices can support the individual exploration of social identity and facilitate intergroup relationships across difference both in the campus ecosystem and in preparation for students' future careers.

The Role of Identity Development and Intergroup Contact in Diversity Competence

That Cross-cultural Psych class ... it really kind of changed my perspective on things. Before I had that class, I had always been used to being the only black person in class, and that continued in college. ... after I took this class, it helped me understand that my experience is personal to me and I have my own personal identification and if I don't act like another black student it's o.k. ... it really helped me become more confident in my own identification. I still struggle with it, because that's how I grew up. But whenever I think, 'Oh I'm not acting a certain way, or like I am acting too white,' I kind of remind myself that there is not one certain way a black person should act. And so I think that's something I became more comfortable with after taking that class. It helped me became more aware of racial identification.

    Tanya, an African-American graduate of a Midwestern public research university

IN THIS CHAPTER, we discuss one of the most critical ways that colleges and universities can affect the ability of undergraduate students to realize the benefits of diversity: through an ecosystem that both fosters the process of identity development and promotes intergroup contact. A campus ecology that promotes active engagement with diversity encourages students to navigate the complexities of their own social identities and interact meaningfully across difference.

Identity is at the heart of the Multicontextual Model for Diverse Learning Environments (MMDLE) discussed in the third chapter in terms of the multiple social identities that students bring to and develop within the institutional microsystem (Hurtado et al., 2012). This conceptual model leads to a further examination of how student identity development can serve as a springboard to working across differences through intergroup relations. The Culturally Engaging Campus Environments (CECE) model specifically addresses the importance of cross-cultural engagement through positive interactions with diverse peers.

A significant body of research has identified the role of intergroup relations and interactional diversity in learning outcomes such as increased empathy, intercultural effectiveness, and intergroup collaboration (see, for example, Bowman, 2013b; Goodman & Bowman, 2014; Gurin et al., 2013). The Intergroup Dialogue (IGD) program developed at the University of Michigan is one of the most prominent models for fostering understanding across differences through inquiry, mutual respect, and empathic connection (Nagda & Gurin, 2007). Further, an important aspect of the IGD program is alliance building among diverse students that, in turn, leads to greater social justice (Gurin et al., 2013).

Recall from the fourth chapter, the progressive learning continuum for diversity, global learning, and civic engagement that begins with the question, "Who am I? (knowledge of self) (Musil, 2009). In this continuum, the process of self-exploration and identity formation leads to a focus on intergroup relations, enhanced civic engagement, and ultimately to the creation of a shared future in a democratic society.

Because identity is one of the most thoroughly investigated areas of social science research (Kim, 2009) and given the significant, recent literature on student identity development (see, for example, Jones & Abes, 2013; Torres, Howard-Hamilton, & Cooper, 2003), we focus on racial/ethnic and lesbian/gay/bisexual/transgender (LGBT) identity development as illustrative of the formative process that can lead to enhanced diversity competence during the undergraduate experience. These aspects of identity formation are particularly salient for minoritized and LGBT college students due to the marginalization, exclusion, and even harassment that can impinge upon their experiences both in society at large and on predominantly white, heterosexually normed campuses. Our purpose is not to recapitulate the extensive literature on student identity development, but rather to provide selected perspectives that illuminate the development of diversity competence supported by the narratives of recent college graduates. These narratives illustrate how the educational experiences of these recent graduates affected their own identity development and diversity competence.

The salience of race and ethnicity coupled with substantive research in this area necessarily brings these prominent dimensions of identity to the forefront on campus (Hurtado et al., 2012). In terms of race and gender, physical identifiability and discrimination work hand in hand to reinforce patterns of discrimination in American society and its institutions (Aguirre & Turner, 1998). Students with invisible stigma such as LGBT individuals must determine whether or not to disclose their identity due to the potential for harassment and devaluation (Chun & Evans, 2012). Students whose gender expression is perceived to violate social norms of male and female identity are also most likely to be victims of sexual harassment on campus, as shown in a 2015 campus climate study of 150,072 students in 27 institutions conducted for the Association of American Colleges and Universities (Cantor et al., 2015).

The Formative College Years and the Social Construction of Identity

The psychologist Erik Erikson indicated that during late adolescence and early adulthood, individuals benefit from a psychosocial moratorium of time and space in which they can experiment with different social roles and develop both personal and social identity (see, for example, Erikson, 1946; Gurin et al., 2002). For this reason, institutions of higher education can serve as a site of psychological moratorium by providing a social milieu that is both diverse and complex and that will encourage intellectual experimentation (Gurin et al., 2002). A range of influences may come into play in this process, including residential arrangements, social networks, faculty-staff mentoring, peer influences, ethnic organizations, and support programs that foster integrated interactions (Museus, 2010).

Earlier in the monograph, we discussed the potential clash between the microsystems of diverse students' everyday experiences and the macro-level systems of inequality. This clash illustrates how the social construction of identity is imposed by the norms, expectations, and stereotypes of the dominant culture, as in the racial or heterosexist stereotypes central to society's framing (Feagin, 2006; Picca & Feagin, 2007). Although all forms of oppression are distinctive historically and socially, not all are of equal significance in a given time or social milieu (Elias & Feagin, in press). Despite such differences, oppression in all its manifestations is similar in construction in terms of power relations that pit and oppressor group against an oppressed group (Elias and Feagin, in press).

The prism of privilege and difference mediates the connections individuals have with different social identities and the relative salience of these identities (Jones & Abes, 2013). Identity salience or the prominence of a particular dimension of identity arises because of the individual's dynamic interaction with larger sociocultural contexts and structures of privilege and oppression (D'Augelli, 1994; Elias & Feagin, in press; Hurtado et al., 2012; Jones & Abes, 2013). Yet forms of oppression are similar in construction in terms of power relations that pit an oppressor group against an oppressed group (Elias & Feagin, in press). Without experiences of difference, privileged identities can remain unscrutinized (Jones & Abes, 2013).

Nearly all the research on identity development, including the nearly 1,000 papers on racial and ethnic identity are based on how people choose and see their identities, not on how they deal with imposed identities, which are more central in a racialized society (J. R. Feagin, personal communication, October 25, 2015). These stereotypes are often repeated in more protected and intimate backstage conversations involving only white men and women, whereas in the frontstage, when diverse individuals are present, a certain performativity and impression management prevails (Picca & Feagin, 2007).

In this regard, our interviewees frequently described the racial epithets, stereotypes complaints, and undertones they heard about various racial groups. For example, Mai, the Asian American graduate of a private Midwestern college cited earlier, noted that she heard stereotypical comments about African-American colleagues as well as comments other students directly made to her, such as, "You got an 'A' because you're an Asian."

For diverse students entering predominantly white institutions, cultural integrity transfers the onus of responsibility from individuals to the institution for recognizing and valuing cultural differences and remedying educational inequality (Tierney, 1999). An important step in fostering cultural integrity is creating an environment in which students are able to develop, affirm, and express their own identity though the power of self-determination and can work across social identities to gain enhanced awareness, knowledge, and skill in intergroup contact.

As we have noted in the first chapter, Kim's (2009) concept of intercultural identity provides a counterpoint to group-based conceptions of cultural identity and reflects an "achieved self-other orientation" developed by an individual over time that is conceived as a continuum of changes moving from a monocultural orientation to increasingly complex and inclusive development (p. 56). This continuum is characterized by two important processes that coincide with identity formation and intergroup contact: individuation or self-definition as a singular individual and universalization or synergistic cognition (Kim, 2009). In the next sections, we address how identity development provides an opportunity for students to move toward self-definition that transcend stereotypical group-based conceptualizations and ultimately leads toward more synergistic intergroup contact.

Racial and Ethnic Identity Formation

The processes of racial and ethnic identity formation among college students have received substantial scholarly attention, including the evolution of a critical consciousness regarding race among white students (Ortiz & Santos, 2009). Critical race theory highlights the role of race and racism as a permanent aspect of American society with hierarchical political, economic, and social structures (DeCuir & Dixson, 2004; Museus, Ravello, & Vega, 2012).

Little research has been conducted on racial identity salience or the level of importance placed by an individual on racial identity, as an outcome of the college experience (Hurtado et al., 2012). Yet studies suggest that it is positively associated with higher academic performance and self-esteem for college students (Hurtado et al., 2012). A study involving 5,010 students at 14 higher education institutions between 2009 and 2010 found clear differences in college students' racial identity salience by racial group (Hurtado et al., 2012). The study confirmed that white students think less about their race than each group of minority students, including Latino/a, Asian American, black, multiracial, and Arab-American students (Hurtado et al., 2012). In addition, regardless of racial background, students who participated more often in campus-facilitated diversity activities, took more classes with materials focused on diversity and equity, or engaged more frequently in conversations outside of class related to racial or ethnic diversity exhibited a higher racial identity salience diversity (Hurtado et al., 2012).

Cross (2012) posits that despite important content differences, different social groups have more similarities than differences in how social identity is enacted in day-to-day interactions. Some of the "underlying social dynamics" of racial development processes are the same and, as a result, discussions about difference can reflect a common language (W. E. Cross, personal communication, February 15, 2016). Based on similarities in the way forms of oppression occurs, Hardiman and Jackson (1997) theorized that racial identity affects how both agents and targets internalize oppression and reorient their relation to members of both agent and target groups in different phases of consciousness. In essence, the dynamics of oppression are similar across its many differing manifestations (Hardiman, Jackson, & Griffin, 2007). Given this commonality of perspective and due to space limitations, we illustrate the elements of a progressive pathway toward racial/ethnic identity development through two representative theories: William Cross' Nigrescence theory that refers to the process of "becoming black" (Cross, 1971, 1991), and Janet Helms' (1993) theory of white racial identity development.

Cross describes the experience of resocializing and transforming black identity in five stages: (a) *preencounter* with the beliefs and values of the dominant white culture; (b) *encounter* with the significance of race and one's own devalued position; (c) *immersion* in the multiplicity of identity; (d) *internalization of a positive identity*; and (e) *internalized commitment* to support the concerns of diverse others (Cross, 1991; see Tatum, 1997 for review). An important aspect of Cross' theory is the distinction made between personal identity and group identity. Blackness is perceived as a social identity or group identity, with personal identity playing only a minor role (Vandiver, Cross, Worrell, & Fhagen-Smith, 2002). Feagin (2013) has particularly emphasized the importance of counterframing or antiracist resistance learning as essential to the process of internalized commitment (Feagin, 2013; Feagin et al., 1996).

With this model in mind, consider how Tanya, an African-American graduate of a large public research university, describes a transformative experience she gained through her cross-cultural psychology course. Although the university did not have a diversity requirement, taking this course helped Tanya realize not only what diversity meant to her but also what it meant to her future aspirations and goals. As she explains, "Growing up I felt my voice was not taken seriously because I was a minority in a school in which all my peers were white." The course helped her shed her former watered-down view of diversity as simply diverse representation and recognize the social justice dimensions of diversity: "It's more than just having a group of different people. It's making sure that everyone in that group has an equal voice or an equal spot to discuss their views." Tanya emphasizes that her experiences in the course gave her a sense of racial identification and differentiation in terms of the fact that she need not conform to stereotypes about her race and could develop her own individual identity and situational responses:

> It [the class] helped me become more aware of racial identification. I became more personally interested in it, and ... become more aware of racial identification issues because I never even thought about that ever being a thing before I took this class. I read articles about racial identification; that's a personal interest for me now. That what helped me become more confident in my own

identification. It's more so how I personally identify as black, even though there might be these stereotypes of how black people act, my personal racial identification of being black is my experiences. That's my own personal identification to me.

Because 60% of the student population in higher education is white (National Center for Education Statistics, n.d.), as reflected also in our survey sample of recent graduates, the development of white racial identity development is key to building more inclusive campus environments in predominantly white institutions. White middle class identity is the dominant identity in American society, with great power to shape other identities (Picca & Feagin, 2007). As a result, the college environment provides the opportunity for white students to examine dominant norms.

Helms' (1993) six-stage theory of white identity development begins with cross-racial contact and culminates in the establishment of a nonracist white identity. This theoretical model views white racial identity as intertwined with the development of consciousness of racism as a system of advantage in the United States and as influenced by contact involving minorities. Like Cross's model, this theory addresses the complexity of gaining independence from predominant social norms by the progressive development of an internalized, integrative perspective. In the process, individuals can experience *dissonance* and disintegration as racism and white privilege become visible, followed by *reintegration* under pressure to conform to social hierarchies and when faced with the cost of opposing racism. Phases of *pseudo-independence* as individuals become aware of racism but do not know what to do about it and *immersion* in antiracist perspectives and history are followed by the attainment of *autonomy* and active engagement in antiracism efforts. Later, Helms modified this stage-based approach to describe "statuses" or more fluid interactions between cognitive and affective practices that allow individuals to participate in more than one status at a time (Helms, 1995; see Renn, 2004 for review). The designation of statuses also avoids the linear nature of stage-based models (Helms, 1995).

In light of Helms' theory, consider how Seth, the gay white male student affairs professional cited earlier, describes the formation of his identity coming from a more sheltered life to a campus learning environment in which he gained a deeper understanding of social inequality:

> *I think that was from just having a more sheltered life in terms of my upbringing, it was very white middle-class, heterosexual, Christian in my immediate family and extended family. And then when I was exposed to all these different people and experiences, that was shocking to me. Some of it was recognizing my privilege, and just grappling with maybe some guilt there, some misunderstanding of how that was in this society. Growing up until 18, I had a very singular view of the world as a place that was much more equal and much more equitable, and that was certainly not the case. I learned that very quickly. So that caused stress. And I remember having conversations and borderline arguments with parents during that time that really challenged them, why did you not expose me to the real world?*

Despite the emphasis of racial identity development on internalization of a positive identity in the face of a dominant culture of white privilege, an emphasis on white privilege and oppression can cause considerable pushback among some white students. Studies indicate that white Americans are more likely to deny the existence of racism in institutional policies and practices than black Americans (Miron, Warner, & Branscombe, 2011). Further, an institutional concept of racism rather than a concept based on the racism of individuals increases awareness of white privilege and constitutes to a threat to group self-image due to the emphasis on unearned advantages (Unzueta & Lowery, 2008).

In this regard, Tatum (1992) points out the importance of processing issues of racial identity and oppression in classroom settings due to the powerful emotional responses that student's experience, ranging from guilt and shame to anger and despair. Unaddressed, these emotional responses can result in resistance to oppression-related content that interferes with cognitive understanding (Tatum, 1992). The process of educating white students about race and racism goes beyond classroom boundaries by changing attitudes and as white students move through their own identity journey they take friends with them (Tatum, 1992). Note, for example, how Paul, a white male graduate of a Midwestern research university, describes his most powerful experience of diversity as an undergraduate as his awareness of white privilege and social injustice:

> *For the sake of being honest—probably comprehending what white privilege is. Not that I could ever truly understand white privilege, but just that I know that it exists and I intentionally, consciously, and obviously unconsciously, take advantage of it as often as possible. I suppose that I take solace knowing that if I can take advantage of the systems we have in place in our country to better and improve my own situation as much as possible at this stage in my life, then perhaps I will have the opportunity and power to help others down the road. Call me selfish and unjust if you want.*

With the increasing number of mixed race students in higher education, research on multiracial identity has increased. Prominent paradigms include Renn's (2000) model of multiracial identity framed in terms of ecological factors such as physical and psychological spaces, peer relations, and identity patterns. Wijeyesinghe's (2001) factor model of multiracial identity (FMMI) is not framed as a stage-based progression but rather includes eight factors that affect choice of racial identity: racial origins, early socialization, cultural attachment, physical appearance, political awareness and orientation, historical and social contexts, spirituality, and the integration of both racial and nonracial social identities. The concept of borderlands is particularly applicable to multiracial students as they navigate the intersections between racial and cultural borders and make meaning of unclear situations and through their own ways of knowing or epistemological growth (Niskode-Dossett & John, 2015).

Sexual and Gender Identity Formation

Beginning in the 1970s, research regarding sexual orientation identity began to emerge in stage-based models that typically begin with a phase of defensive strategies that attempt to minimize same-gender feelings culminating in integration of a nonheterosexual identity as lesbian or gay as a positive self-identity (Bilodeau & Renn, 2005). A first step in the formation of gay, lesbian, bisexual, or transgender identity is "coming out" or openly acknowledging same-sex attractions and proclaiming one's identity (Rhoads, 1994). Such self-acknowledgment is a revolutionary act by repudiating a majority identity and making sexual orientation visible (D'Augelli, 1994). The context imposing public identity is critical and can support inclusion or, conversely, create a sense of profound alienation.

In contrast to essentialist approaches that view identity as typically achieved at a certain point in chronological time, a life-span approach to sexual orientation emphasizes developmental plasticity (D'Augelli, 1994). Because of normative cultural expectations, being lesbian, gay, or bisexual involves a life characterized by multiple psychological identities in the face of powerful socially imposed barriers and penalties (D'Augelli, 1994). For example, a 2003 study of 14 campuses with 1,669 participants, including 719 GLBT undergraduates, and 281 GLBT graduate students found that 27% of the GLBT respondents indicated that they were closeted or out to only a few family members (Rankin, 2003). GLBT respondents from minority groups were more likely than white GLBT people to conceal their sexual orientation out of fear of harassment (Rankin, 2003). Although some institutions have provided structural support for sexual and gender identity development through GLBT resource centers, student groups, resident assistant sensitivity training, and safe space programs, even on these campuses the climate has not been welcoming (Rankin, 2003). As a result, such plasticity in conditions suggests that sexual identity development is responsive to environmental circumstances over the course of the life span, is malleable, sometimes transient, and prolonged (D'Augelli, 1994).

Rhoads (1994) proposes an ethnic model of gay identity in which ethnicity denotes a group identification that individuals are born with or socialized to adopt. Based on a study of 40 gay and bisexual men at an Eastern research university, Rhoads describes the ongoing socialization process that occurs on campus as students engage actively in the everyday social life of the university with culture as a guiding framework. Gay students engage in a nonheterosexual counterculture of shared understandings and "social collectivity" through ongoing interactions—some of which are defined in opposition to the dominant culture—as they experiment with and forge a sense of identity (Rhoads, 1994, p. 35). This cultural orientation in the process of socialization is consistent with the ecological theories of person–environment interaction described earlier in the monograph.

Increasing scholarly recognition of the diversity of sexual orientation has found clear differences in the ways that bisexuals experience identity from the ways in which lesbian or gay individuals do (Bilodeau & Renn, 2005). In the area of gender identity, transgender identity development describes the individual's determination of a male, female, or identity outside or between these two categories (Bilodeau & Renn, 2005). The term "queer," although contested and sometimes politicized, is a unifying umbrella term that describes all lesbian, gay, and bisexual individuals (Rhoads, 1994) and more recently includes transgendered and intersex persons, including those questioning their own sexual and gender identities.

Holistic Perspectives on Identity Development

Earlier in the monograph, we have touched on intersectionality as a formative aspect of cultural identity. Recent research increasingly emphasizes the holistic, integrated development of the multiple facets of identity rather than the discrete treatment of singular dimensions (Jones & Abes, 2013). As a result, identity development involves not only racial and ethnic identity development but also encompasses other aspects of difference and the integration of more than a single dimension of identity, including sexual minority, gender, disability, and religious identities among others (see, for example, Bilodeau & Renn, 2005; Buggie-Hunt, 2007; Jones & McEwen, 2000; McEwen, 2003; Nettles & Balter, 2012; Reynolds & Pope, 1991; Ross, 2005). In addition, attention needs to be directed toward within-group differences and their impact on identity development (Reynolds & Pope, 1991).

The intersection of race, class, gender, sexual orientation, and other identity markers and the interrelatedness of racialized, gendered, and classed social institutions pose unique challenges for students during the formative college period (Elias & Feagin, in press). Building on seminal work on multiple layers of identity within the context of student identity development (Jones & McEwen, 2000; Reynolds & Pope, 1991), the Multi-dimensional Identity Model (MMDI) provides a conceptualization of three factors: (a) a core sense of self in terms of guiding personal beliefs and relational, inclusive values; (b) context that includes inequitable power structures, family background, and cultural factors; and (c) multiple social identities (Jones & Abes, 2013). The holistic process of identity development can be strengthened through structured intergroup contact on college campuses in which students have an opportunity to examine their own positionality and work collaboratively across differences.

Structured Intergroup Contact

Structured intergroup contact on college campuses plays a dual role in serving as an avenue for enhanced identity development both for white students and for members of nondominant groups who face imposed identity pressures and those who are less obviously phenotyped such as mixed race students. Such structured contact provides an experiential crucible for forging meaningful intergroup relationships.

Intergroup practices draw upon the four conditions in Allport's (1954) intergroup contact theory for reducing prejudice: (a) equal status between groups; (b) common goals; (c) intergroup cooperation; and (d) support of relevant authorities (Allport, 1954; Gurin Nagda, & Zuniga et al., 2013; Pettigrew & Tropp, 2005). In addition, since Allport's definitive theory was introduced, additional aspects of contact that reduce prejudice have been identified: personal friendships, especially when these relationships involve nonstereotypic elements, and intergroup friendships (Dovidio, Eller, & Hewstone, 2011).

A meta-analytic study involving 713 independent samples from 515 studies reveals that although Allport's conditions for intergroup contact serve as significant, facilitating factors in prejudice reduction, these conditions are not essential in producing these outcomes (Pettigrew & Tropp, 2006). In fact, researchers found that institutional support may serve as an especially important criterion for attaining positive contact results when taken in consideration with other factors (Pettigrew &Tropp, 2006). Recent research also reveals the importance of familiarity to breed "liking," resulting in the reduction of uncertainty and feelings of anxiety and threat in intergroup contact (Pettigrew & Tropp, 2006). As a result, empathy and perspective taking are critical factors in reducing prejudice, with affective mediators playing a more important role than cognitive mediators (knowledge) (Pettigrew, 2008). In fact, strategies that examine emotions and feelings such as imagining how outgroup members feel have been especially effective in reducing intergroup prejudice (Tropp & Pettigrew, 2005).

The most successful and empirically verifiable practice for structured intergroup contact directly related to the educational process is the IGD program developed at the University of Michigan beginning in 1989 with the first formal curricular offering. Implemented widely at many universities and often as a credit-bearing course, IGD has resulted in a proliferation of research and practitioner-based literature. Whereas diversity education works within existing social structures to strengthen understanding and social justice education emphasizes the need for greater social structural equality to prepare students for participation in culturally diverse societies, IGD explicitly addresses interactions among different social identity groups in the classroom (Nagda & Gurin, 2007). It involves a critical dialogic approach composed of three components: (a) understanding and analysis of dominance and difference; (b) discursive engagement across difference; and (c) sustained and collaborative community building and conflict resolution (Nagda & Gurin, 2007). As such, the practice of IGD promotes active and engaged learning through structured interaction in facilitated learning environments (Nagda, Gurin, Sorensen, & Zúñiga, 2009).

While early approaches focused more on prejudice reduction and intergroup harmony, later development of the program emphasized social identity, in-group solidarity and group consciousness as a resource for collective action (Gurin et al., 2013). In making identity a prominent focus, IGD assumes a multicultural rather than a color-blind approach that recognizes inequality as a significant influence on social and life experiences (Nagda et al. 2009). Especially pertinent to this monograph are the contributions that IGD can make through the application of research-based knowledge to the challenges of intergroup relations in the contemporary world (Gurin et al., 2013). As such, IGD represents a democratic and transformative approach to learning about social inequality, social identities, and social change (Nagda & Maxwell, 2011). The IGD opens channels of communication and creates bridges between individuals who have affected by the unequal distribution of power (Nagda & Gurin, 2007). In this sense, it offers both the opportunity for learning about others and political understanding (Nagda & Gurin, 2007).

The process of intergroup dialogue involves structured interactions that bring together equal numbers of students from at least two identity groups who meet for several hours each week over a sustained time period of 10 to 14 weeks (Nagda et al., 2009). Two co-facilitators, one from each identity group, guide the process through structured activities using reflection, integration of content, and dialogic communication (Nagda et al., 2009). Students thoughtfully examine how power structures create and reproduce inequality and explore ways in which they can contribute collectively to greater social justice (Gurin et al., 2013). The process of dialogue strives for mutual understanding, not agreement and, unlike the oppositional process of debate, views differences as a means of encouraging inquiry and reappraising perspectives rather than as points of division (Gurin et al., 2013; Nagda et al., 2009).

A collaborative study of nine universities that includes 26 race/ethnicity dialogues and 26 control groups as well as 26 gender dialogues with 26 control groups validates the learning outcomes provided by intergroup dialogue. Students in the dialogue groups as compared to the control groups showed greater identity engagement, greater motivation to bridge differences, greater increases in empathy, and increased motivation to influence political structures and be engaged in postcollege communities focused on social policy (Nagda et al., 2009). In addition, participants in the IGD program gained increased confidence in taking action and actual behaviors, as well as greater responsibility for challenging others who make derogatory comments about other groups (Nagda et al., 2009).

The Program on Intergroup Relations at the University of Michigan hosts an annual National Intergroup Dialogue Institute each year to help institutions support and develop academic and cocurricular programs ("National Intergroup Dialogue Institute," 2015). Dialogue programs are implemented in four basic structural models: stand-alone courses for academic credit; components of a larger course; field experiences; and cocurricular offerings (Zúñiga, Nagda, Chesler, & Cytron-Walker, 2007).

In addition to IGD programs, some campuses have structured conversations around diversity issues such as Colby College's Campus Conversations on Race (CCOR) that began in 2007 based on a model borrowed from Emerson College. In this program, faculty advisors train student cofacilitators, who then pair up to lead 6-week student-only discussion groups focused on racial identity issues (Okoh & de Sherbinin, n.d.). At Colby, too, a month-long, intensive winter-term course titled "Multicultural Literacy" attracts 80 to 100 students each year. The course was designed to teach first-year students the vocabulary and conceptual framework needed to understand how privilege works about social class, race, ethnicity, ability, gender, and sexual orientation. It models the move from dialogue to action by requiring community projects. CCOR and "Multicultural Literacy" have been shown to feed enrollments in related courses and majors, increase attendance at diversity events, and "have made a palpable impact on the level of sophistication with which students conduct public discourse, query visiting speakers, and participate on college-wide committees." (J. de Sherbinin, personal communication, February 12, 2016). Through these efforts, Colby College has made significant strides toward the ideals of inclusion and equality in these efforts to move campus culture ahead and foster enhanced diversity competence (J. de Sherbinin, personal communication, February 12, 2016).

Another structured program designed to foster meaningful dialogue around social identity issues is the national Sustained Dialogue program that emphasizes a dialogue-to-action process. At Montana State University, for example, the program takes place over a 15-week period with groups of 8 to 12 students and two facilitators. The program is designed to increase awareness of identity, promote interactions across difference, and create a more inclusive campus environment. Other related activities include a 3-day Common

Ground retreat of 30 students that allows the participants to further explore identity differences in an off-campus setting (A. Donohue, personal communication, February 22, 2016).

Concluding Observations

The college years represent a crucial and formative period in terms of identity development and intergroup contact, leading to enhanced capacity for diversity awareness and competence. Although the literature on identity development is extensive, leading theorists have identified the common psychological dynamics that underpin different manifestations of oppression, the similar ways in which social identity is enacted in day-to-day interactions, and the importance of counter-framing in response to socially-imposed norms as part of the developmental process of internalized commitment (Cross, 2012; Feagin, 2013; Hardiman & Jackson, 1997; Hardiman et al., 2007).

We have noted how the experiences of marginalization and exclusion are particularly salient for minoritized and LGBT students on predominantly white, heterosexually normed campuses. For students from nondominant groups such as minoritized and LGBT students, the process of identity development often requires discarding socially imposed identities and engaging in a continuous, lifelong process of self-acceptance, intergroup collaboration, and affirmation. In light of the dominance of white, middle-class social norms, we have shared examples of white racial identity formation and provided examples of how the ecosystem can help white students who have been less conscious of racial identity to develop an antiracist identity. Tatum's caution that resistance to discussions of oppression and privilege can arise in the classroom and lead to anger, denial and even guilt is important in understanding emotional reactions to such topics.

Recent holistic identity models offer the opportunity for integration of different facets of identity rather than emphasis on a singular dimension. Consider how Tracey, the white female graduate of an isolated western research university cited earlier, describes her most powerful experience of diversity as when a white, female instructor opened the door in class discussions for the few African-American students to share their experiences. These discussions led the class to come to a common understanding about race and what it means to have an intersectional identity encompassing more than a singular dimension of difference. As Tracey explains, "this was a profound moment for me."

Across many campuses, inadequate resources and attention are devoted to support for identity development and structured intergroup communication. In fact, most of our survey participants did not identify any campus programs or resources that had helped them in this area. The research cited in this chapter demonstrates that structured programs that emphasize meaningful contact among individuals from different social identities over a sustained period of time can enhance empathy and perspective taking through practices that emphasize both cognitive and affective strategies. Thoughtful and intentional planning is a necessary precursor to the development and availability of integrated programs and resources that support student identity development and intergroup contact in the campus ecosystem.

Strategies and Recommendations for Practice

But it's also just coming from my experience at my college, the backlash that occurs the moment you bring race into a situation with people who have never had to think about their race. The backlash that we received was predominantly anonymous. We would have events for black history month, in one event we chose the menu and decorations for the dining halls, and people, instead of embracing another culture, would make racist comments. The more that we tried to bring up diversity there seemed to a lot of backlash from the student body . . . people who never had to think about race and are being forced to, and instead of using this as a learning experience, they got angry. . . . It's just very disheartening. Even though a lot of members were deeply hurt, even to the point of tears from all the crazy things that happened and things that were said from the largely white student body, backlash is what, in order to be a pioneer for change, you have to deal with.

Kiara, an African-American research technician and graduate of a private Eastern liberal arts college

KIARA, A NATIVE of Africa who grew up in the United States, describes her experiences in leading a student organization for black and Hispanic students on a predominantly white campus and the backlash she and her colleagues received whenever race was brought into the picture. Her narrative underscores the ways in which students can serve as change agents and pioneers in diversity progress. Kiara notes how her leadership experiences as president of the student organization strengthened her skills and competence in navigating a diverse workplace:

> *I learned many lessons from being a minority on a college campus. Lessons lost to my white peers who don't have to be placed in a group where they are the minority. Lessons necessary to survive in a diverse world. My college experience enabled me to successfully navigate talking to people of different races, without prejudice, whereas other people might struggle with that. I've also learned the importance of leaving your comfortable racially homogeneous circle to interact and learn from others unlike you.*

Kiara's commentary presents a compelling example of the distance that predominantly white institutions still need to go to create inclusive environments and cultivate diversity competence among the student body. We have noted in this monograph the discomfort associated with discussions of issues of social stratification, oppression, and privilege. Yet as our exploration of the meaning of diversity competence reveals, culture necessarily involves the interrelationships of social identity, culture, and power as well as historical legacies of inequality and systemic discrimination (Feagin, 2013; Halualani & Nakayama, 2013).

Although the Supreme Court has affirmed the educational benefits of diversity as a "compelling state interest," this legal determination is only a starting point and naturally raises the practical question of how such benefits can be realized. Further, the shift from remedial to nonremedial affirmative action with the diversity rationale focuses simplistically on the benefits that white students and all other students obtain from policies originally intended to address the long history of white preference (Orfield, 2001). The educational benefits of diversity need also to address the social and institutional legacies of exclusion, discrimination, and marginalization. For this reason, as research has shown, simply increasing the diversity of the student body will not, by itself, lead to meaningful engagement across difference and will require thoughtful planning.

Our interviews with recent college graduates indicate that students were often unaware of their institution's diversity mission or if they were aware of it, they described a significant disconnect between espoused and lived diversity values. Some were fortunate enough to find a faculty mentor in a single course who engaged them in a deeper understanding of power and privilege. Others identified their most powerful diversity experience as serving as resident adviser, due to the need to interact with demographically diverse students. More often than not, students had to seek out the experiences of diversity as undergraduates and often could not identify a single transformative diversity program, interaction, or event.

We have also identified a number of promising approaches in this monograph that can lead to an integrated and holistic experience of diversity during the undergraduate experience. At some institutions, however, even a single diversity course in the general education curriculum has raised significant opposition. Other universities offer such a wide array of courses to satisfy a single diversity course requirement that it is unclear whether students will have the opportunity to gain a broad-based, holistic understanding of diversity issues. In such cases, students may perceive a diversity curricular requirement as simply a check-box process without investment in the learning outcomes. In essence, the development of diversity competence is an integral part of the learning process and cannot simply be viewed as an add-on to general education curricular requirements.

In addition, we have explored the reasons why diversity competence has not been systematically addressed in the undergraduate experience. Clearly, one of the most significant reasons is that cultural or diversity competence is not well defined. Faculty may see it as an amorphous subject, lacking in disciplinary rigor, and not an essential part of the undergraduate curriculum. At the same time, unlike the helping and healthcare professions such as medicine, nursing, dental education, public health, counseling, and social work, most accreditation processes do not directly address cultural competence or require accountability for its attainment. As a result, there is a tendency to view diversity competence as a luxury or an appendage to the educational process, something nice-to-have but not necessary. Further, such competence is associated with pleasant events such as international potlucks and is often devoid of consideration of the problematic social issues of inequality and social justice.

Several highly promising developments are, however, reshaping the landscape for the attainment of diversity competence. First, the Association of American Colleges and Universities has assumed a prominent role in describing the goals of a liberal education in terms of democratic learning outcomes. The "LEAP" ("Liberal Education and America's Promise") framework described in the third chapter emphasizes intercultural knowledge and competence as an essential learning outcome. Three of the 16 LEAP VALUE rubrics for undergraduate education directly relate to the attainment of diversity competence through Intercultural Knowledge and Competence, Global Learning, and Civic Engagement. Second, the Degree Qualifications Profile for associate's, bachelor's, and master's degrees developed under the auspices of the Lumina Foundation, emphasizes civic and global learning as one of the five categories of learning outcomes and emphasizes broad, integrative knowledge. One of the most promising developments in launching the Degree Qualifications Profile was the pilot undertaken by the Higher Learning Commission of its new Open Pathway accreditation model, a model that emphasizes the institution's role in a multicultural society and the need for students to understand the human and cultural diversity of the world in which they live and work. Third, the diversity mapping methodology that visually portrays how diversity is actualized on a campus and includes an extensive curricular inventory provides a powerful tool for gauging the extent to which diversity is addressed in multiple aspects of the college experience. All of these developments underscore the critical importance of diversity competence and its tie to learning outcomes and the ability of students to navigate in a diverse, interconnected society.

In concluding the monograph, we offer the following specific suggestions for campuses seeking to systematically address diversity competency in the undergraduate experience and within the campus ecosystem as a whole.

Build an Overarching Academic and Administrative Infrastructure for Diversity Competence

- *Ensure multilevel support for a holistic diversity infrastructure emanating from the board of trustees and the president and including the faculty senate, administrators, faculty, and staff.* Examples of best practices shared in the monograph illustrate the critical role of university leadership in driving diversity change as well as the importance of broad-based buy-in and advocacy across the institution.

- *Develop a common definition of diversity competence and include as a goal for student learning and development that is addressed in institutional mission statement and strategic planning documents.* As we have noted, one of the principal difficulties in building an ecology for diversity competence lies in arriving at a common definition of such competence. In addition, few institutions have included the attainment of diversity or cultural competence as a goal in their overall institutional mission statements or in the desired learning outcomes for students. In general, colleges and professional schools associated with the helping professions are the only areas of the university that have done so.

- *Use the organizing frameworks of the Multicontextual Model for Diverse Learning Environments (MMDLE) and Culturally Engaging Campus Environments (CECE) models shared in the third chapter to address the ways in which the campus provides a holistic environment for diversity learning outcomes and the attainment of student success* (Hurtado & Guillermo-Wann, 2013; Museus, 2014). *Engage in an overall comprehensive diversity assessment using these frameworks.* The climate assessment that measures key concepts in the MMDLE is nationally available through the Higher Education Research Institute at the University of California at Los Angeles and has already been used by over 60 institutions to foster institutional change (Hurtado & Guillermo-Wann, 2014). The CECE website at the University of Denver offers research, tools, and resources that enable campuses to engage in concrete strategic approaches that will create more welcoming environments for diverse students (http://www.du.edu/cece-project/). In addition, the visual mapping methodology that has been implemented at more than 20 universities offers the opportunity for specific assessment of evolutionary progress in diversity engagement throughout the campus ecosystem (Hurtado & Halualani, 2014).

- *Draw upon the conceptual principles of inclusive excellence as a change model that incorporates diversity or cultural competence and prepares students for citizenship in a diverse society.* Missouri State University (MSU) represents a prominent example of the implementation of a systemic inclusive excellence model that has been made possible through sustained leadership at both the institutional and faculty and staff levels. The university's statewide public affairs mission is composed of three pillars: ethical leadership, cultural competence, and community engagement. The goal of the public affairs mission is to differentiate the educational experience at Missouri State from other institutions and to educate students to imagine the future (Missouri State University, 2013). The pairing of the public affairs mission that focuses on cultural competence with the inclusive excellence change model establishes both the goal and the mechanism for structural, institutional change.

- The institution was one of the four participating universities in Harvard University's Voice of Diversity (VoD) project referenced earlier in the monograph and the only one whose president, Michael Nietzel, requested that its participation be made public (Caplan & Ford, 2014). MSU had a history until the middle of the 20th century of refusing to admit black students and is located in Springfield, Missouri, a geographical area of the country with one of the highest percentages of white residents (Caplan & Ford, 2014). The VoD follow-up with the university has been ongoing and resulted in significant changes, including the president's proposal to the board of governors to prioritize diversity and create a vice president for diversity and inclusion position (Caplan & Ford, 2014).

- Prior to the VoD study, an Inclusive Excellence (IE) Work Group composed of faculty and staff was formed to develop guidelines for the university's long-range planning process. The work group addressed four perspectives: Access and Equity, Campus Climate, Student Learning and Development, and Diversity in the Formal and Informal Curriculum that were to be addressed in an Inclusive Excellence Plan and Change Model for all divisions and units (Missouri State University, 2010). Recommendations of the work group and the President's Commission for Diversity were incorporated in Missouri State's 2011–2016 Long-Range Plan that includes three enduring, overarching commitments: student learning, inclusive excellence, and institutional impact (Missouri State University, 2014).

- This collaborative effort by faculty and staff stakeholders represents a model of working in systematic ways across all areas, with the public affairs mission of the university as a leverage point (L. Anderson, personal communication, February 15, 2016). In the words of Professor Leslie Anderson, former chair of the IE Work Group, "I have often said that the pillars of the public affairs mission must begin with cultural competence, since there is neither ethical leadership nor true community engagement without it" (L. Anderson, personal communication, February 15, 2016).
- *In creating structured and balanced conditions for students from diverse backgrounds, consider the implications for different racial/ethnic groups including multiracial students.* As shared in the monograph, despite an increase in the number of multiracial students, campus practices that address these students are still relatively few. Rather than a monolithic approach, greater attention needs to be paid to the differing needs of diverse student groups (Clarke & Antonio, 2012).
- *Survey recent college graduates to determine their perspectives on how the college or university's diversity mission may or may not have been actualized.* In the interviews we conducted, recent graduates offered substantive insights into how the college or university could have strengthened the diversity mission and experiences. Unfortunately, in some cases, graduates could not recall a single, powerful experience of diversity, and some indicated simply that they were unaware of their institution's diversity mission. The perspectives of recent graduates are an important and often untapped resource on how to enhance the educational experience of diversity.

Establish Student Learning Outcomes that Enhance Diversity Competence

- *Conduct an audit of how diversity is embodied across the curriculum and cocurricular programs.* In the fifth chapter, we shared models that provide a basis for a campus wide inventory of curricular offerings with diversity content as well as best practice examples. Nelson Laird's (2011, 2014) model of diversity inclusivity offers a way of evaluating different components of diversity in both required and non-required courses. As part of the audit, consideration needs to be given to which disciplines have made significant headway in diversity inclusivity.

- *Explicitly address the need for diversity or cultural competence as a learning outcome in the undergraduate curriculum and tie this outcome to the need for students to navigate as citizens in a diverse, global society.* Consider, for example, how the University of Maryland College Park's mission statement articulates the goal of cultural competence in its objectives for undergraduate education: "The General Education curriculum provides students with opportunities to develop cultural competence, to recognize human differences and to appreciate their value in plural societies" (University of Maryland, 2014).

- *Enlist faculty leadership in addressing diversity competence within the curriculum.* The instrumental role of faculty leadership through taskforces, collaborative workgroups, and faculty senate committees has been noted in several examples shared in the monograph.

- *Use first-year experiences to promote diversity during the most formative period of the undergraduate college experience.* Because the research literature shared in this monograph clearly identifies the first year as pivotal in student experiences of diversity, ensure that first-year experiences and programs provide the opportunity for sustained diversity interactions and development of diversity competence.

- *Incorporate the emphasis on diversity competence in admissions processes and materials as well as student orientation programs.* Review admissions materials, processes, and new student orientation programs to ensure that students understand the integral connection of diversity competence to the educational process and institutional mission.

Strengthen Faculty and Staff Hiring, Evaluation, and Professional Development Processes to Include the Need for Diversity Competence

- Include diversity competence in position descriptions and job postings. The definition of cultural competence offered by Pope, Reynolds, and Mueller (2004) refers specifically to the awareness, knowledge, and skills needed to effectively communicate, collaborate, and engage with others who are different from oneself in meaningful ways through interactions characterized by reciprocity, mutual understanding, and respect.
- Provide comprehensive professional development offerings in diversity competence for administrators, faculty, and staff.
- Recognize contributions to diversity engagement in evaluation processes and recognition programs.

Enhance the Resources Available to Support Student Identity Development and Intergroup Learning

- Evaluate the ways in which the college or university addresses student identity development for both majority and minoritized students. In the sixth chapter, we discussed the importance of student identity development as the springboard for diversity competence. Often campuses do not provide sufficient resources or attention to the crucial and formative process of identity development, particularly for minoritized students on predominantly white campuses.
- Faculty and administrators may not view this facet of the student experience as falling under their purview or may assume that student affairs is addressing it. One of the campuses with several students participating in our survey offers significant help to students in the process of identity development through the Women's Studies program. Other interviewees cited a single professor who assisted them. However, in most cases, opportunities for such mentoring were unplanned, accidental, and relied on student initiative. As a result, an overall evaluation of opportunities and support for student identity development would be valuable including but not limited to resources such as counseling centers, faculty mentoring, ethnic and women studies programs, ethnic organizations, student leadership programs, and safe zones. Further, recognition and reward programs for

faculty mentors who have led the way in support student identity development will create further incentive for building a supportive infrastructure.

- *Address the heterogeneity of the student body and its diverse needs through structured intergroup learning that promotes perspective taking, reciprocal understanding, and social justice.* The most prominent practice for intergroup
learning that promotes cross-group interactions in a classroom setting is
the Intergroup Dialogue Program from the University of Michigan. This
program promotes authentic dialogue across difference while recognizing
the impact of power structures on the creation and reproduction of inequality and helping students think about ways to contribute to social justice.
Often offered through the curriculum, this program enhances the ability of
students to work proactively across difference in support of social change.

Foster Inclusive Pedagogical Practices

- *Develop strategies for addressing classroom diversity and creating culturally inclusive classroom environments.* A number of students described the pressure
from situations in which diverse students might be asked in classroom settings to be role models for their race. Andrew, a marine sciences graduate of
a southern research university, who came from a white middle-class background, described the impact of a relatively diverse campus on broadening
his perspectives: "Increased cultural diversity in my life has made me more
open to all viewpoints and beliefs, and made me more aware of prejudices
that people from different backgrounds than myself face." At the same time,
in classroom settings, Andrew experienced situations in which minorities
were made to be the spokespersons for their race. As a result, Andrew suggests that greater incorporation of diversity into course offerings may reduce
the pressure on diverse individuals in predominantly white classrooms to
represent their ethnic backgrounds:

> *For the most part classes were either predominantly black or pre-
> dominantly white. And that may be because of certain courses of
> study that people have chosen, or just randomly, or because I was
> in Marine Sciences because traditionally there are not a lot of
> African-American students. . . . It does put a lot of pressure on*

them. . . . but if colleges provide courses that include descriptions of diversity and their importance, I think that can reduce the social pressures on students might place on students who are not well represented based on their diverse backgrounds.

A recent incident at Mount Holyoke College in which a professor singled out specific minoritized students in his class to name slurs used against their own racial groups illustrates how classroom situations can reproduce discrimination and inequality and create painful repercussions for these students. In a discussion of Robinson Crusoe, an English professor, Eugene Hill, sought to illustrate the use of the word "papist" as a derogatory term and called on minoritized students to explicitly identify these slurs (Flaherty, 2015). He allegedly asked an African-American student, Danielle Brown, to name a slur for African Americans. As she reported, "My mind was racing but physically, I was frozen" she wrote. "How do I react to this?" (Flaherty, 2015). Although she debated leaving class, she answered that she didn't know the slur. According to her account, the professor forced her to respond, but she would only say "negro" and added, "We get what you're saying. Just drop i–," and the professor then allegedly said, "Nigger! I would say nigger" (Flaherty, 2015). Seven students immediately transferred out of the section as a result of this insensitively personalized incident (Flaherty, 2015).

As we have seen throughout the monograph, the evolutionary journey toward the creation of a holistic campus ecosystem that builds diversity competence has just begun on many campuses. Our interviews with students from all backgrounds on predominantly white campuses indicate the urgent need for systematic institutional attention to the attainment of diversity competence. As Kiara emphasized at the opening of this chapter, diversity competence is necessary for survival in a diverse society, and students who realize the educational benefits of diversity benefit from cross-group interactions will benefit immeasurably from these experiences both during their undergraduate years as well as in their future careers.

Strategies for building a holistic and inclusive learning environment for the attainment of student diversity competence in higher education would benefit from the "edge" effect described by cellist Yo-Yo Ma. This biological phenomenon involves the ability to transcend physical limitations in a transition zone where two ecosystems meet, such as the forest and savannah, and where the greatest diversity flourishes (Huizenga, 2013), As Ma explains:

> *The edge effect is where those of varied backgrounds come together in a zone of transition: a region of less structure, more diversity and more possibility. The edge is a time and place of transformation and movement.*

In conclusion, diversity or cultural competence can provide students with the edge effect needed to learn, live, and thrive in a diverse, multicultural world, and build the groundwork that activates their deep, sustained, and transformative interactions with individuals from different social identities and backgrounds. In a world divided by culturally induced stereotypes, power inequities, and artificial demographic barriers, diversity competence gives the new generation of learners a clear edge: the ability to see beyond difference into the hearts of others and to transform collective experiences into a mutually reinforcing vision of reality.

Note

1. The term "minoritized" is used instead of minority to denote the socially constructed reproduction of inequality that "renders" and subordinates individuals from underrepresented racial/ethnic groups as minorities within the context of predominantly white campus environments (Harper, 2012b, p. 9).

References

Adelman, C., Ewell, P., Gaston, P., & Schneider, C. G. (2011). *The Degree Qualifications Profile: Defining degrees—A new direction for American higher education to be tested and developed in partnership with faculty, students, leaders and stakeholders.* Indianapolis, IL: Lumina Foundation for Education.

Aguirre, A., Jr., & Martinez, R. O. (2002). Leadership practices and diversity in higher education: Transitional and transformational frameworks. *Journal of Leadership Studies, 8*(3), 53–62.

Aguirre, A., Jr., & Martinez, R. O. (2007). Diversity leadership in higher education [*ASHE-ERIC Higher Education Report, 32*(3)] San Francisco, CA: Jossey-Bass.

Aguirre, A., & Turner, J. (1998). *American ethnicity: The dynamics and consequences of discrimination* (2nd ed.). New York: McGraw-Hill.

Allport, G. W. (1954). *The nature of prejudice.* Cambridge, MA: Addison-Wesley.

Allport, G. W. (1979). *The nature of prejudice* (25th ed.). New York: Perseus Books.

Amerson, R. (2010). The impact of service-learning on cultural competence. *Nursing Education Perspective, 31*(1), 18–22.

Appiah, K. A. (1994). Identity, authenticity, survival: Multicultural societies and social reproduction. In C. Taylor, K. A. Appiah, J. Habermas, S. C. Rockefeller, M. Walzer, & S. Wolf., *Multiculturalism: Examining the politics of recognition* (pp. 149–164). Princeton, NJ: Princeton University Press.

Argyris, C. (1994). The future of workplace learning and performance. *Training and Development, 48*(5), 36–47.

Arnold, K. D., Lu, E. C., & Armstrong, K. J. (2012). The ecology of college readiness [*ASHE Higher Education Report, 38*(5)]. San Francisco, CA: Jossey-Bass.

Association of American Colleges and Universities (AAC&U). (2007). *College learning for the new global century: A report from the national leadership council for liberal education & America's promise.* Retrieved from https://www.aacu.org/sites/default/files/files/LEAP/GlobalCentury_final.pdf

Association of American Colleges and Universities (AAC&U). (2015). *High-impact, integrative general education at Northern Illinois University.* (2015). Retrieved from http://aacu.org/campus-model/high-impact-integrative-general-education-northern-illinois-university

Association of American Colleges and Universities (AAC&U). (n.d.-a). LEAP Campus Action Network. Retrieved from https://www.aacu.org/leap/can

Association of American Colleges and Universities (AAC&U). (n.d.-b). VALUE rubrics. Retrieved from https://www.aacu.org/value-rubrics

Astin, A. W. (1997). Liberal education and democracy: The case for pragmatism. In R. Orrill (Ed.), *Education and democracy: Re-imagining liberal learning in America* (pp. 207–224). New York: College Entrance Examination Board.

Astin, A. W., Vogelgesang, L. J., Ikeda, E. K., & Yee, J. A. (2000). *How service learning affects students.* Retrieved from www.heri.ucla.edu/PDFs/HSLAS/HSLAS.PDF

Banks, J. A. (1976). The emerging states of ethnicity: Implications for staff development. *Educational Leadership, 34*(3), 190–193.

Banks, J. A. (1993). Approaches to multicultural curriculum reform. In J. A. Banks & C. A. McGee Banks (Eds.), *Multicultural education: Issues and perspectives* (pp. 195–214). Boston: Allyn & Bacon.

Banks, J. A. (1995). Multicultural education and curriculum transformation. *Journal of Negro Education, 64*(4), 390–400.

Banks, J. A. (1998). The lives and values of researchers: Implications for educating citizens in a multicultural society. *Educational Researcher, 27*(7), 4–17.

Banks, J. A. (2008). Diversity, group identity, and citizenship education in a global age. *Educational Researcher, 37*(3), 129–139.

Bell, L. A. (2016). Theoretical foundations for social justice education. In M. Adams, L. A. Bell, & P. Griffin (Eds.), *Teaching for diversity and social justice: A sourcebook* (3rd ed., pp. 3–26). New York: Routledge.

Bersin, J. (2012). *Building the agile enterprise: A new model for HR.* Retrieved from http://www.slideshare.net/jbersin/impact-2012-keynote-josh-bersin

Bersin, J. (2014). *The new model for talent management: Agenda for 2015.* Retrieved from http://www.slideshare.net/jbersin/talent-management-revisited

Bilodeau, B. L., & Renn, K. A. (2005). Analysis of LGBT identity development models and implications for practice. In R. L. Sanlo (Ed.), *New Directions for Student Services: No. 111. Gender identity and sexual orientation: Research, policy, and personal perspectives* (pp. 25–39). San Francisco, CA: Jossey-Bass.

Bond, M. A., & Haynes, M. C. (2014). Workplace diversity: A social-ecological framework and policy implications. *Social Issues and Policy Review, 8*(1), 167–201.

Bowman, N. A. (2009). College diversity courses and cognitive development among students from privileged and marginalized groups. *Journal of Diversity in Higher Education, 2*(3), 182–194.

Bowman, N. A. (2010a). College diversity experiences and cognitive development: A meta-analysis. *Review of Educational Research, 80*(1), 4–33.

Bowman, N. A. (2010b). Disequilibrium and resolution: The nonlinear effects of diversity courses on well-being and orientations toward diversity. *Review of Higher Education, 33*(4), 543–568.

Bowman, N. A. (2011). Promoting participation in a diverse democracy: A meta-analysis of college diversity experiences and civic engagement. *Review of Educational Research, 81*(1), 29–68.

Bowman, N. A. (2012). Promoting sustained engagement with diversity: The reciprocal relationships between informal and formal college diversity experiences. *Review of Higher Education, 36*(1), 1–24.

Bowman, N. A., (2013a). How much diversity is enough? The curvilinear relationship between college diversity interactions and first-year student outcomes. *Research in Higher Education, 54*(8), 874–894.

Bowman, N. A. (2013b). The conditional effects of interracial interactions on college student outcomes. *Journal of College Student Development, 54*(3), 322–328.

Bowman, N. A., & Brandenberger, J. W. (2012). Experiencing the unexpected: Toward a model of college diversity experiences and attitude change. *Review of Higher Education, 35*(2), 179–205.

Boyle-Baise, M. (2002). *Multicultural service learning: Educating teachers in diverse communities.* New York: Teachers College Press.

Bronfenbrenner, U. (1976). The experimental ecology of education. *Educational Researcher, 5*(9), 5–15.

Bronfenbrenner, U. (1977). Toward an experimental ecology of human development. *American Psychologist, 32*(7), 513–531.

Bronfenbrenner, U. (1979). *The ecology of human development: Experiments by nature and design.* Cambridge, MA: Harvard University Press.

Bronfenbrenner, U. (1995). Developmental ecology through space and time: A future perspective. In P. Moen, G. H. Elder, & K. Lüscher (Eds.), *Examining lives in context: Perspectives on the ecology of human development* (pp. 619–647). Washington, DC: American Psychological Association.

Bronfenbrenner, U., & Morris, P. A. (2006). The bioecological model of human development. In R. M. Lerner (Ed.), *Handbook of child psychology* (pp. 793–828). Hoboken, NJ: Wiley.

Bruce, A. (2012). *Co-curricular diversity transcript: Promising practices information on fostering interaction and integration.* Retrieved from http://go.sdsu.edu/strategicplan/files/01154-DIV_Co_Curricular_Transcript_information_9-21-2012.pdf

Buggie-Hunt, T. (2007). *Psychosocial and disability identity development among college students with disabilities* (Unpublished doctoral dissertation). State University of New York, Buffalo.

Burke, M. (2013). *Colorblindness vs. race-consciousness—An American ambivalence.* Retrieved from http://thesocietypages.org/specials/colorblindness-vs-race-consciousness/

Butin, D. W. (2006). The limits of service-learning in higher education. *Review of Higher Education, 29*(4), 473–498.

Butin, D. (2010). *Service-learning in theory and practice: The future of community engagement in higher education.* New York: Palgrave MacMillan.

Campus Compact. (2015). *Service-learning: Initiatives: Service-learning.* Retrieved from http://compact.org/initiatives/service-learning/

Cantor, D., Fisher, B., Chibnall, S., Townsend, R., Lee, H., Bruce, C., & Thomas, G. (2015). *Report on the campus climate survey on sexual assault and sexual misconduct.* Washington, DC: Association of American Universities. Retrieved from https://www.aau.edu/uploadedFiles/AAU_Publications/AAU_Reports/Sexual_Assault_Campus_Survey/Report

%20on%20the%20AAU%20Campus%20Climate%20Survey%20on%20Sexual%20Ass
ault%20and%20Sexual%20Misconduct.pdf

Caplan, P. J., & Ford, J. C. (2014). The voices of diversity: What students of diverse races/ethnicities and both sexes tell us about their college experiences and their perceptions about their institutions' progress toward diversity. *APORIA, 6*(3), 30–69.

Chang, M. J. (2002). The impact of undergraduate diversity course requirement on students' racial views and attitudes. *Journal of General Education, 51*(1), 21–42.

Chang, M. J. (2007). Beyond artificial integration: Reimagining cross-racial interactions among undergraduates. In S. R. Harper & L. D. Patton (Eds.), *New Directions for Student Services: No. 120. Responding to the realities of race on campus* (pp. 25–37). San Francisco, CA: Jossey-Bass.

Chang, M. J. (2011). *Quality matters: Achieving benefits associated with racial diversity.* Retrieved from http://kirwaninstitute.osu.edu/wp-content/uploads/2012/09/Mitchell-Chang_final_Nov.-1-2011_design_3.pdf

Chang, M. J. (2013). Post-Fisher: The unfinished research agenda on student diversity in higher education. *Educational Researcher, 42*(3), 172–173.

Chang, M. J., Astin, A. W., & Kim, D. (2004). Cross-racial interaction among undergraduates. Some consequences, causes, and patterns. *Research in Higher Education, 45*(5), 527-551.

Chang, M. J., Chang, J. C., & Ledesma, M. C. (2005). Beyond magical thinking: Doing the real work of diversifying our institutions. *About Campus, 10*(2), 9–16.

Chang, M. J., Denson, N., Sáenz, V., & Misa, K. (2006). The educational benefits of sustaining cross-racial interaction among undergraduates. *Journal of Higher Education, 77*(3), 430–455.

Chesler, M. A., Lewis, A., & Crowfoot, J. (2005). *Challenging racism in higher education: Promoting justice.* Lanham, MD: Rowman & Littlefield.

Chun, E. (2013). *Meet our nation's first-generation college students.* Retrieved from http://www.insightintodiversity.com/wp-content/media/issues/november2013.pdf

Chun, E., & Evans, A. (2009). Bridging the diversity divide: Globalization and reciprocal empowerment in higher education [*ASHE-ERIC Higher Education Report*,35(1)]. San Francisco, CA: Jossey-Bass.

Chun, E., & Evans, A. (2012). *Diverse administrators in peril: The new indentured class in higher education.* Boulder, CO: Paradigm Publishers.

Chun, E., & Evans, A. (2015). Affirmative action at a crossroads: Fisher and forward [*ASHE-ERIC Higher Education Report, 41*(4)]. San Francisco, CA: Jossey-Bass.

Chun, J. K. (1985). *The relation to education of guilt and conscience in the philosophy of Soren Kierkegaard and Martin Heidegger* (Unpublished doctoral dissertation). Columbia University.

Clarke, C. G., & Antonio, A. L. (2012). Rethinking research on the impact of racial diversity in higher education. *Review of Higher Education, 36*(1), 25–50.

Clayton-Pedersen, A., & Musil, C. M. (2005). Introduction to the series. In D. A. Williams, J. B. Berger, & S. A. McClendon (Eds.), *Toward a model of inclusive excellence and change in postsecondary institutions* (pp. iii–ix). Washington, DC: Association of American Colleges & Universities. Retrieved from http://www.aacu.org/inclusive_excellence/documents/williams_et_al.pdf

Clayton-Pedersen, A. R., Parker, S., Smith, D. G., Moreno, J. F., & Teraguchi, D. H. (2007). *Making a real difference with diversity: A guide to institutional change.* Washington, DC: Association of American Colleges and Universities.

Collins, P. H. (1993). Learning from the outsider within: The sociological significance of black feminist thought. In J. S. Glazer-Raymo, E. M. Bensimon, & B. K. Townsend (Eds.), *Women in higher education: A feminist perspective* (pp. 45–64). Needham Heights, MA: Ginn Press.

Cook, B. J., (2012). *The American college president study: Key findings and takeaways.* Retrieved from http://www.acenet.edu/the-presidency/columns-and-features/Pages/The-American-College-President-Study.aspx

Cox, T., & Beale, R. L. (1997). *Developing competency to manage diversity: Readings, cases & activities.* San Francisco: Berrett-Koehler Publishers.

Cross, W. (1991). *Shades of black: Diversity in African American identity.* Philadelphia, PA: Temple University.

Cross, W. E. (1971). The Negro to Black conversion experience: Toward a psychology of black liberation. *Black World, 20,* 13–71.

Cross, W. E. (2012). The enactment of race and other social identities during everyday transactions. In In C. L. Wijeyesinghe & B. W. Jackson (Eds.), *New perspectives on racial identity development: A theoretical and practical anthology* (pp. 191–215). New York: New York University Press.

Dartmouth College. (2013). *Transformative learning.* Retrieved from http://strategicplanning.dartmouth.edu/strategic-opportunities

D'Augelli, A. R. (1994). Identity development and sexual orientation: Toward a model of lesbian, gay, and bisexual development. In E. J. Trickett, R. J. Watts, & D. Birman (Eds.), *Human diversity: Perspectives on people in context* (pp. 312–333). San Francisco, CA: Jossey-Bass.

Deardorff, D. K. (2009). Synthesizing conceptualizations of intercultural competence: A summary and emerging themes. In D. K. Deardorff (Ed.), *The SAGE handbook of intercultural competence* (pp. 264–270). Thousand Oaks, CA: SAGE Publications.

Deardorff, D. K. (2011). Assessing intercultural competence. In J. D. Penn (Ed.), *New Directions for Institutional Research: No. 149. Assessing complex general education student learning outcomes* (pp. 65–79). San Francisco: CA: Jossey-Bass.

Decker Lardner, E. (2003). *Approaching diversity through learning communities* (Occasional paper no. 2). Olympia, WA: Washington Center for Improving the Quality of Undergraduate Education. Retrieved from http://www.evergreen.edu/washingtoncenter/docs/diversityoccpaper.pdf

DeCuir, J. T., & Dixson, A. D. (2004). "So when it comes out, they aren't that surprised that it is there": Using critical race theory as a tool of analysis of race and racism in education. *Educational Researcher, 33*(5), 26–31.

Denson, N. (2009). Do curricular and co-curricular diversity activities influence racial bias? A meta-analysis. *Review of Educational Research, 79,* 805–836.

Denson, N., & Chang, M. J. (2009). Racial diversity matters: The impact of diversity-related student engagement and institutional context. *American Educational Research Journal, 46*(2), 322–353.

Denson, N., & Chang, M. J. (2015). Dynamic relationships: Identifying moderators that maximize benefits associated with diversity. *Journal of Higher Education, 86*(1), 1–37.

Dey, E. L. & Hurtado, S. (1995). College impact, student impact: A reconsideration of the role of students within American higher education. *Higher Education, 30*(2), 207–223.

Dey, E. L., Ott, M. C., Antonaros, M., Barnhardt, C. L., & Holsapple, M. A. (2010). *Engaging diverse viewpoints: What is the campus climate for perspective-taking?* Retrieved from https://www.aacu.org/publications-research/publications/engaging-diverse-viewpoints-what-camp us-climate-perspective

Dovidio, J. F., Eller, A., & Hewstone, M. (2011). Improving intergroup relations through direct, extended and other forms of indirect contact. *Group Processes Intergroup Relations, 14*(2), 147–160.

Dovidio, J. F., Gaertner, S. L., Stewart, T. L., Esses, V. M., ten Vergert, M., & Hodson, G. (2004). From intervention to outcome: Processes in the reduction of bias. In W. G. Stephan & W. P. Vogt (Eds.), *Education programs for improving intergroup relations: Theory, practice, and research* (pp. 243–266). New York: Teachers College Press.

Elias, S., & Feagin, J. R. (in press). *Racial theories in the social sciences: A systemic racism critique.* New York: Routledge.

Eller, J. D. (2015). *Culture and diversity in the United States: So many ways to be American.* New York: Routledge.

Emerson College. (2015). *Inclusive excellence: Values & competencies.* Retrieved from http://www.emerson.edu/about-emerson/offices-departments/diversity/student-staff-faculty-resou rces/values-competencies

Engberg, M. E. (2007). Educating the workforce for the 21st century: A cross-disciplinary analysis of the impact of the undergraduate experience on students' development of a pluralistic orientation. *Research in Higher Education, 48*(3), 283–317.

Erikson, E. H. (1946). Ego development and historical change. *Psychoanalytic Study of the Child, 2*, 359–396.

Evans, A., & Chun, E. B. (2007). Are the walls really down? Behavioral and organizational barriers to faculty and staff diversity [*ASHE-ERIC Higher Education Report, 33*(1)]. San Francisco, CA: Jossey-Bass.

Fay, D. B. (2015). *Multinational customers: Are their needs really being met?* Retrieved from http://www.globexintl.com/corporate/?p=82

Feagin, J. R. (2006). *Systemic racism: A theory of oppression.* New York: Routledge.

Feagin, J. R. (2013). *The white racial frame: Centuries of racial framing and counter-framing* (2nd ed.). New York: Routledge.

Feagin, J. R., & O'Brien, E. (2003). *White men on race: Power, privilege, and the shaping of cultural consciousness.* Boston: Beacon Press.

Feagin, J. R., Vera, H., & Imani, N. (1996). *The agony of education: Black students at white colleges and universities.* New York: Routledge.

Ferber, A. L., & Herrera, A. (2005). Teaching diversity and fostering inclusivity at the university: A collaborative approach. In M. L. Ouellett (Ed.), *Teaching inclusively: Resources for course, department and institutional change in higher education* (pp. 152–162). Stillwater, OK: New Forums Press.

Flaherty, C. (2015). *Race and slurs in the classroom.* Retrieved from https://www.insi dehighered.com/news/2015/10/05/incident-mount-holyoke-renews-debate-talking-about-raceclassrooms

Flannery, D., & Ward, K. (1999). Service learning: A vehicle for developing cultural competence in health education. *American Journal of Health Behavior, 23*, 323–331.

Florida State University. (n.d.). *Social justice living learning community.* Retrieved from http://thecenter.fsu.edu/Programs/Social-Justice-Living-Learning-Community

Frank, J. R., Snell, L. S., Cate, O. T., Holmboe, E. S., Carraccio, C., Swing, S. R., Harris, P., ... Harris, K. A. (2010). Competency-based medical education: Theory to practice. *Medical Teacher, 32*(8), 638–645.

Frank, S. (2014, December 18). Only 54 UCLA professors sign petition against UCLA racism. Retrieved from http://www.capoliticalreview.com/ capoliticalnewsand-views/only-54-ucla-professors-sign-petition-against-ucla-racism/

Freedman, J. O. (2003). *Liberal education and the public interest.* Iowa City, IA: University of Iowa Press.

Garrett, N. (n.d.). *Note to the Senate Membership from Legislative Assembly Secretary Professor Neal Garrett.* Retrieved from http://www.senate.ucla.edu/documents/ProConSummaryFinal.pdf

Garrod, A., Kilkenny, R., & Gómez, C. (Eds.). (2013). *Mixed: Multiracial college students tell their life stories.* Ithaca, NY: Cornell University Press.

Gaston, P. L. (2015). *General education transformed: How we can, why we must.* Washington, DC: Association of American Colleges and Universities.

Giroux, H. A., & Giroux, S. S. (2004). *Take back higher education: Race, youth, and the crisis of democracy in the post-civil rights era.* New York: Palgrave Macmillan.

Goodman, K. M., & Bowman, N. A. (2014). Making diversity work to improve college student learning. In G. L. Martin & M. S. Hevel (Eds.), *New Directions for Student Services: No. 147. Research-driven practice in student affairs: Implications from the Wabash National Study of Liberal Arts Education* (pp. 37-48). San Francisco, CA: Jossey-Bass.

Goodman, L. A., Liang, B., Helms, J. E., Latta, R. E., Sparks, E., & Weintraub, S. R. (2004). Training counseling psychologists as social justice agents: Feminist and multicultural principles in action. *Counseling Psychologist, 32*(6), 793–837.

Gurin, P. (1999). *Expert report of Patricia Gurin.* Retrieved from http://diversity.umich.edu/admissions/legal/expert/gurintoc.html

Gurin, P., Dey, E. L., Hurtado, S., & Gurin, G. (2002). Diversity and higher education: Theory and impact on educational outcomes. *Harvard Educational Review, 72*(3), 330–366.

Gurin, P., Nagda, B. (R). A., & Lopez, G. E. (2004). The benefits of diversity in education for democratic citizenship. *Journal of Social Issues, 60*(1), 17–34.

Gurin, P., Nagda, B. (R). A., & Zúñiga, X. (2013). *Dialogue across difference: Practice, theory and research on intergroup dialogue.* New York: Russell Sage Foundation.

Guthrie, K. L., Jones, T. B., Osteen, L. K., & Hu, S. (2013). Cultivating leader identity and capacity in students from diverse backgrounds [*ASHE-ERIC Higher Education Report, 39*(4)]. San Francisco, CA: Jossey-Bass.

Gutmann, A. (1994a). Introduction. In A. Guttman (Ed.), *Multiculturalism: Examining the politics of recognition* (pp. 3–24). Princeton, NJ: Princeton University Press.

Gutmann, A. (1994b). Preface. In A. Guttman (Ed.), *Multiculturalism: Examining the politics of recognition* (pp. ix–xii). Princeton, NJ: Princeton University Press.

Halualani, R. T. (2011). In/visible dimensions: Framing the intercultural communication course through a critical intercultural communication framework. *Intercultural Education, 22*(1), 43–54.

Halualani, R. T., Haiker, H., & Lancaster, C. (2010). Mapping diversity efforts as inquiry. *Journal of Higher Education Policy and Management, 32*(2), 127–136.

Halualani, R. T., Haiker, H. L., Lancaster, C., & Morrison, J. H. (2015). *Diversity mapping data portrait*. Retrieved from https://csumb.edu/sites/default/files/images/st-block-95-1429229970817-raw-csumbdiversitymappingdataportrait.pdf

Halualani, R. T., Haiker, H., & Thi, J. H. (2013). *PennState: A comprehensive evaluation and benchmarking*. Retrieved from http://equity.psu.edu/workshop/assets/pdf/fall13/penn-state-comprehensive-evaluation-infographics

Halualani, R. T., & Nakayama, T. K. (2013). Critical intercultural communication studies: At a crossroads. In T. K. Nakayama & R. T. Halualani (Eds.), *Handbook of critical intercultural communication* (pp. 1–16). Malden, MA: Blackwell Publishing.

Hammer, M. R. (2009). The intercultural development inventory: An approach for assessing and building intercultural competence. In M. A. Moodian (Ed.), *Contemporary leadership and intercultural competence: Exploring the cross-cultural dynamics within organizations* (pp. 203–218). Thousand Oaks, CA: SAGE Publications.

Hammer, M. R. (2012). The intercultural development inventory: A new frontier in assessment and development of intercultural competence. In M. V. Berg, R. M. Paige, & K. H. Lou (Eds.), *Student learning abroad: What our students are learning, what they're not, and what we can do about it* (pp. 115–136). Sterling, VA: Stylus Publishing.

Hammer, M. R., Bennett, M. J., & Wiseman, R. (2003). Measuring intercultural sensitivity: The intercultural development inventory. *International Journal of Intercultural Relations, 27*(4), 421–443.

Hardiman, R., & Jackson, B. W. (1997). Conceptual foundation for social justice courses. In M. Adams, L. A. Bell, & P. Griffin (Eds.), *Teaching for diversity and social justice: A sourcebook*, (pp.16–29). New York: Routledge.

Hardiman, R., Jackson, B. W., & Griffin, P. (2007). Conceptual foundations for social justice education. *Teaching for diversity and social justice: A sourcebook* (2nd ed., pp. 35–66). New York: Routledge.

Harper, S. R. (2012a). *Foreword*. In S. D. Museus & U. M. Jayakumar (Eds.), *Creating campus cultures: Fostering success among racially diverse student populations* (pp. ix–xi). New York: Routledge.

Harper, S. R. (2012b). Race without racism: How higher education researchers minimize racist institutional norms. *Review of Higher Education, 36*(1), 9–29

Harper, S. R., & Hurtado, S. (2007). Nine themes in campus racial climates and implications for institutional transformation. In S. R. Harper & L. D. Patton (Eds.), *New Directions for Student Services: No. 120. Responding to the realities of race on campus* (pp. 7–24). San Francisco, CA: Jossey-Bass.

Harper, S. R., & Quaye, S. J. (2009). Beyond sameness, with engagement and outcomes for all: An introduction. In S. R. Harper & S. J. Quaye (Eds.), *Student engagement in higher education: Theoretical perspectives and practical approaches for diverse populations* (pp. 1–16). New York: Routledge.

Harris, J. C., BrckaLorenz, A., & Laird, T. F. N. (2014). *Engaging in the margins: Exploring differences in biracial students' engagement by racial/ethnic makeup*. Paper presented at the Association for the Study of Higher Education Conference, Washington, DC. Retrieved from http://nsse.iub.edu/pdf/presentations/2014/ASHE14BiracialPaper_Final.pdf

Hart Research Associates. (2015). *Falling short? College learning and career success*. Retrieved from https://www.aacu.org/sites/default/files/files/LEAP/2015employerstudentsurvey.pdf

Helms, J. E. (1993). Toward a model of white racial identity development. In J. E. Helms (Ed.), *Black and white racial identity: Theory, research, and practice* (pp. 49–66). New York: Praeger.

Helms, J. E. (1995). An update of Helms's white and people of color racial identity models. In J. G. Ponterotto, J. M. Casas, L. Suzuki, & C. M. Alexander (Eds.), *Handbook of multicultural counseling* (pp. 181–198). Thousand Oaks, CA: Sage Publications.

Higher Learning Commission (HLC). (2015a). *Policy title: Criteria for accreditation*. Retrieved from http://policy.hlcommission.org/Policies/criteria-for-accreditation.html

Higher Learning Commission (HLC). (2015b). *Systems portfolio structure*. Retrieved from http://www.hlcommission.org/Pathways/aqip-overview.html

Higher Learning Commission (HLC). (2015c). *The criteria for accreditation: Guiding values*. Retrieved from https://www.hlcommission.org/Criteria-Eligibility-and-Candidacy/guiding-values.html

Higher Learning Commission (HLC). (2015d). *The quality initiative: Institutional improvement in the open pathway*. Retrieved from http://www.hlcommission.org/Pathways/quality-initiative.html

Housman, J., Meaney, K. S., Wilcox, M., & Cavazos, A. (2012). The impact of service-learning on health education students' cultural competence. *American Journal of Health Education, 43*(5), 269–278.

Howard, C. C. (1992). *Theories of general education: A critical approach*. New York: St. Martin's Press.

Howard, M. A. (2014). Foreword. In National Survey of Student Engagement, *Bringing the Institution into Focus—Annual Results 2014* (pp. 2–3). Bloomington, IN: Indiana University Center for Postsecondary Research.

Huizenga, T. (2013). *Can Yo-Yo Ma fix the arts?* Retrieved from http://www.npr.org/sections/deceptivecadence/2013/04/09/176681242/can-yo-yo-ma-fix-the-arts

Hurtado, S. (1992). The campus racial climate: Contexts of conflict. *Journal of Higher Education, 63*(5), 539–569.

Hurtado, S., & Alvarado, A. R. (2015). Realizing the potential of Hispanic-serving institutions: Multiple dimensions of organizational transformation. In A-M. Núñez, S. Hurtado, & E. C. Galdeano (Eds.), *Hispanic-serving institutions: Advancing research and transformative practice* (pp. 25–46). New York: Routledge.

Hurtado, S., Alvarado, A. R., & Guillermo-Wann, C. (2012). *Inclusive learning environments: Modeling a relationship between validation, campus climate for diversity, and sense of belonging.* Paper presented at the Annual Conference of the Association for Studies in Higher Education, Las Vegas, Nevada. Retrieved November 29, 2015, from http://www.heri.ucla.edu/ford/downloads/ASHE2012-Inclusive-Learning.pdf

Hurtado, S., Alvarez, C. L., Guillermo-Wann, C., Cuellar, M., & Arellano, L. (2012). A model for diverse learning environments: The scholarship on creating and assessing conditions for student success. In J. C. Smart & M. B. Paulsen (Ed.), *Higher education: Handbook of theory and research* (Vol. 27, pp. 41–122). New York: Springer.

Hurtado, S., & DeAngelo, L. (2012). Linking diversity and civic-minded practices with student outcomes: New evidence from national surveys. *Liberal Education, 98*(2), 14–23.

Hurtado, S., Griffin, K. A., Arellano, L., & Cuellar, M. (2008). Assessing the value of climate assessments: Progress and future directions. *Journal of Diversity in Higher Education, 1*(4), 204–221.

Hurtado, S., & Guillermo-Wann, C. (2013). *Diverse learning environments: Assessing and creating conditions for student success—Final report to the Ford Foundation.* Los Angeles, CA: Higher Education Research Institute, University of California, Los Angeles. Retrieved from http://www.heri.ucla.edu/ford/DiverseLearningEnvironments.pdf

Hurtado, S., & Halualani, R. (2014). Diversity assessment, accountability, and action: Going beyond the numbers. *Diversity and Democracy, 17*(4), Retrieved from https://www.aacu.org/diversitydemocracy/2014/fall/hurtado-halualani

Hurtado, S., Milem, J. F., Clayton-Pedersen, A. R., & Allen, W. R. (1998). Enhancing campus climates for racial/ethnic diversity: Educational policy and practice. *Review of Higher Education, 21*(3), 279–302.

Hurtado, S., Milem, J. F., Clayton-Pedersen, A. R., & Allen, W. R. (1999). Enacting diverse learning environments: Improving the climate for racial/ethnic diversity in higher education [*ASHE-ERIC Higher Education Report,* 26(8)]. Washington, DC: The George Washington University.

Institute-wide task force on the future of MIT education: Final report. (2014). Retrieved from http://web.mit.edu/future-report/TaskForceFinal_July28.pdf

Jaschik, S. (2015, April 13). UCLA faculty approves diversity requirement. Retrieved from https://www.insidehighered.com/news/2015/04/13/ucla-faculty-approves-diversity-requirement

Jayakumar, U. M. (2008). Can higher education meet the needs of an increasingly diverse and global society? Campus diversity and cross-cultural workforce competencies. *Harvard Educational Review, 78*(4), 615–651.

Jayakumar, U. M., & Museus, S. D. (2012). Mapping the intersection of campus cultures and equitable outcomes among racially diverse student populations. In S. D. Museus and U. M. Jayakumar (Eds.), *Creating campus cultures: Fostering success among racially diverse student populations* (pp. 1–27). New York: Routledge.

Johnson, Y. M., & Munch, S. (2009). *Fundamental contradictions in cultural competence.* Retrieved from http://sw.oxfordjournals.org/content/54/3/220.abstract

Jones, N. A., & Bullock, J. (2012). *The two or more races population: 2010.* Washington, DC: Census Bureau. Retrieved from http://www.census.gov/prod/cen2010/briefs/c2010br-13.pdf

Jones, S. R., & Abes, E. S. (2013). *Identity development of college students: Advancing frameworks for multiple dimensions of identity.* San Francisco, CA: Jossey-Bass.

Jones, S. R., & McEwen, M. K. (2000). A conceptual model of multiple dimensions of identity. *Journal of College Student Development, 41*(4), 405–414.

Kennedy, R. (2013). *For discrimination: Race, affirmative action, and the law.* New York: Pantheon.

Kezar, A. J. (2001). Understanding and facilitating organizational change in the 21st century: Recent research and conceptualizations [*ASHE-ERIC Higher Education Report,* 28(4)]. San Francisco, CA: Jossey-Bass.

Kezar, A. (2002). Reconstructing static images of leadership: An application of positionality theory. *Journal of Leadership & Organizational Studies, 8*(3), 94–109.

Kezar, A. (2005). What do we mean by "learning" in the context of higher education? In A. Kezar (Ed.), *New Directions for Higher Education: No. 131. Organizational learning in higher education* (pp. 49–59). San Francisco, CA: Jossey-Bass.

Kezar, A., & Carducci, R. (2009). Revolutionizing leadership development: Lessons from research and theory. In A. Kezar (Ed.), *Rethinking leadership in a complex, multicultural, and global environment: New concepts and models for higher education* (pp. 1–38). Sterling, VA: Stylus.

Kezar, A. J., & Eckel, P. D. (2005). *Leadership strategies for advancing campus diversity: Advice from experienced presidents.* Washington, DC: American Council on Education.

Kezar, A., Eckel, P., Contreras-McGavin, M., & Quaye, S. J. (2008). Creating a web of support: An important leadership strategy for advancing campus diversity. *Higher Education, 55*(1), 69–92.

Kim, Y. Y. (2009). The identity factor in intercultural competence. In D. K. Deardorff (Ed.), *The SAGE handbook of intercultural competence* (pp. 53–65). Thousand Oaks, CA: SAGE Publications.

Kimball, B. A. (1997). Naming pragmatic liberal education. In R. Orrill (Ed.), *Education and democracy: Re-imagining liberal learning in America* (pp. 45–68). New York: College Entrance Examination Board.

King, P. M., & Baxter Magolda, M. B. (2005). A developmental model of intercultural maturity. *Journal of College Student Development, 46*(6), 571–592.

King, J., & Gomez, G. G. (2008). *On the pathway to the presidency: Characteristics of higher education's senior leadership.* Washington, DC: American Council on Education.

Kitano, M. K. (1997). What a course will look like after multicultural change. In M. I. Morey & M. K. Kitano (Eds.). *Multicultural course transformation in higher education: A broader truth* (pp. 18–34). Boston: Allyn and Bacon.

Knefelkamp, L., & Schneider, C. (1997). Education for a world lived in common with others. In R. Orrill (Ed.), *Education and democracy: Re-imagining liberal learning in America* (pp. 327–351). New York: College Entrance Examination Board.

Krishnamurthi, M. (2005). Institutional transformation to support inclusive teaching initiatives. In M. L. Ouellett (Ed.), *Teaching inclusively: Resources for course, department and institutional change in higher education* (pp. 258–271). Stillwater, OK: New Forums Press.

Kuh, G. D., Kinzie, J., Buckley, J. A., Bridges, B. K., & Hayek, J. C. (2007). Piecing together the student success puzzle: Research, propositions, and recommendations [*ASHE-ERIC Higher Education Report, 32*(5)]. San Francisco, CA: Jossey-Bass.

Kuh, G. D., & Whitt, E. J. (1988). The invisible tapestry: Culture in American colleges and universities [*ASHE-ERIC Higher Education Report, 17*(1)]. San Francisco, CA: JosseyBass.

Ladson-Billings, G. (2013). Critical race theory—What it is not! In M. Lynn & A. D. Dixson (Eds.), *Handbook of critical race theory in education* (pp. 34–47). New York: Routledge.

Lederman, D. (2012). *The (aging) college president.* Retrieved from https://www.insidehighered.com/news/2012/03/12/college-presidents-are-older-whiter-more-likely-come-outside-academe

Lee, A., Poch, R., Shaw, M., & Williams, R. D. (2012). Engaging diversity in undergraduate classrooms: A pedagogy for developing intercultural competence [*ASHE-ERIC Higher Education Report, 38*(2)]. San Francisco, CA: Jossey-Bass.

Leiter, W. M., & Leiter, S. (2011). *Affirmative action in antidiscrimination law and policy: An overview and synthesis* (2nd ed.). Albany, NY: State University of New York.

Levin, J. S., Jackson-Boothby, A., Haberler, Z., & Walker, L. (2015). "Dangerous work": Improving conditions for faculty of color in the community college. *Community College Journal of Research and Practice, 39*(9), 1–13.

Lobst, W. (2009). *Competency-based medical education: The basics.* Retrieved from http://sites.duke.edu/medicaleducationgrandrounds/files/2012/11/GR-Duke-2-4-13.pdf

Lumina Foundation. (2014). *The Degree* Qualifications Profile: A learning-*centered framework for what college graduates should know and be able to do to earn the associate, bachelor's or master's degree.* Indianapolis, IN: Author. Retrieved from https://www.luminafoundation.org/files/resources/dqp.pdf

McEwen, M. K. (2003). New perspectives on identity development. In S. R. Komives., D. B. Woodard, Jr., & Associates (Eds.), *Student services: A handbook for the profession* (4th ed., pp. 203–233). San Francisco, CA: Jossey-Bass.

McKenna, M. J., & Ward, K. (1996). Service learning: A culturally relevant pedagogy. *Thresholds in Education, 22,* 18–22.

Meaney, K. S., Bohler, H. R., Kopf, K., Hernandez, L., & Scott, L. S. (2008). Service-learning and pre-service educators' cultural competence for teaching: An exploratory study. *Journal of Experiential Education, 31*(2), 189–208.

Melnick, S. L. (2000). Multiculturalism: One view from the United States of America. In B. Moon, M. Ben-Peretz, & S. A. Brown (Eds.), *Routledge international companion to education* (pp. 456–475). New York: Routledge.

Menand, L. (1997). Re-imagining liberal education. In R. Orrill (Ed.), *Education and democracy: Re-imagining liberal learning in America* (pp. 1–20). New York: College Entrance Examination Board.

Mendoza, S. L., Halualani, R. T., & Drzewiecka, J. A. (2002). Moving the discourse on identities in intercultural communication: Structure, culture, and resignifications. *Communication Quarterly, 50*(3–4), 312–327.

Middle States Commission on Higher Education. (2015). *Standards for accreditation and requirements of affiliation* (13th ed.). Philadelphia, PA: Author. Retrieved from http://www.msche.org/publications/RevisedStandardsFINAL.pdf

Milem, J. F. (2003). The educational benefits of diversity: Evidence from multiple sectors. In M. Chang, D. Witt, J. Jones, & K. Hakuta (Eds.), *Compelling interest: Examining the evidence on racial dynamics in colleges and universities* (pp. 126–169). Stanford, CA: Stanford University Press.

Milem, J. F., Chang, M. J., & Antonio, A. L. (2005). *Making diversity work on campus: A research-based perspective.* Retrieved from https://siher.stanford.edu/making-diversity-work-campus-research-based-perspective

Miller, K. L., & Toma, J. D. (2011). What does it mean to act affirmatively in hiring processes? Diversity as a strategic imperative in higher education. In P. M. Magolda & M. B. Baxter Magolda (Eds.), *Contested issues in student affairs: Diverse perspectives and respectful dialogue* (pp. 262–272). Sterling, VA: Stylus Publishing.

Miron, A. M., Warner, R. H., & Branscombe, N. R. (2011). Accounting for group differences in appraisals of social inequality: Differential injustice standards. *British Journal of Social Psychology, 50*(2), 342–353.

Missouri State University. (2010). *2011–2016 long-range strategic planning process: Inclusive excellence workgroup: Draft report.* Retrieved from http://www.missouristate.edu/assets/longrangeplan/PPT_2_Anderson.pdf

Missouri State University. (2013). *Pillars of public affairs.* Retrieved from http://publicaffairs.missouristate.edu/Pillars.htm

Missouri State University. (2014). *2011–2016 long-range plan: Fulfilling our promise.* Retrieved from http://www.missouristate.edu/longrangeplan/commitments.htm.

Mont, E., Shorter-Gooden, K., Stevens, C., & Nash, P. T. (2015, May 29). *Cultural competence in undergraduate education: A case study on how to make it happen.* Paper presented at the 2015 National Conference on Race and Ethnicity, Washington, DC.

Moon, D. G. (2010). Critical reflections on culture and critical intercultural communication. In T. K. Nakayama & R. T. Halualani (Eds.), *The handbook of critical intercultural communication* (pp. 34–52). Malden, MA: Blackwell Publishing.

Museus, S. D. (2008). Focusing on institutional fabric: Assessing campus cultures to enhance cross-cultural engagement. In S. R. Harper (Ed.), *Creating inclusive campus environments for cross-cultural learning and student engagement* (pp. 205–234). Washington, DC: National Association of Student Personnel Administrators.

Museus, S. D. (2010). Delineating the ways that targeted support programs facilitate minority students' access to social networks and development of social capital in college. *Enrollment Management Journal, 4*(3), 10–41.

Museus, S. D. (2014). The culturally engaging campus environments (CECE) model: A new theory of success among racially diverse college student populations. In M. B. Paulsen (Ed.), *Higher education: Handbook of theory and research,* (Vol. 29, pp. 189–227). New York: Springer

Museus, S. D., & Griffin, K. A. (2011). Mapping the margins in higher education: On the promise of intersectionality frameworks in research and discourse. In K. A. Griffin and S. D. Museus (Eds.), *Using mixed methods to study intersectionality in higher education* (pp. 5–14). Hoboken, NJ: John Wiley & Sons, Inc.

Museus, S. D., & Harris, F. (2010). Success among college students of color: How institutional culture matters. In T. E. Dancy (Ed.), *Managing diversity: (Re)visioning equity on college campuses* (pp. 25–44). New York: Peter Lang.

Museus, S. D., Lam, S. C., Huang, C. Y., Kem, P., & Tan, K. (2012). Cultural integration in campus subcultures: Where the cultural, academic, and social spheres of college life collide. In S. D. Museus & U. M. Jayakumar (Eds.), *Creating campus cultures: Fostering success among racially diverse student populations* (pp. 106–129). New York: Routledge.

Museus, S. D., Nichols, A. H., & Lambert, A. D. (2008). Racial differences in the effects of campus racial climate on degree completion: A structural equation model. *The Review of Higher Education, 32*(1), 107–134.

Museus, S. D., Ravello, J. N., & Vega, B. E. (2012). The campus racial culture: A critical race counterstory. In S. D. Museus & U. M. Jayakumar (Eds.), *Creating campus cultures: Fostering success among racially diverse student populations* (pp. 28–45). New York: Routledge.

Museus, S. D., & Yi, V. (2015). Rethinking student involvement and engagement: Cultivating culturally relevant and responsive contexts for campus participation. In. D. Mitchell Jr, K. M. Soria, E. A. Daniele, & J. A. Gipson (Eds.), *Student involvement and academic outcomes: Implications for diverse college student populations* (pp. 11–24). New York: Peter Lang.

Musil, C. M. (2003). Educating for citizenship. *Peer Review, 5*(3), 4–8.

Musil, C. M. (2009). Educating students for personal and social responsibility: The civic learning spiral. In B Jacoby & Associates (Ed.), *Civic Engagement in higher education: Concepts and practices* (pp. 49–68). San Francisco: Jossey-Bass.

Musil, C. M. (2011). Reconfiguring civic engagement on campus: What are the levers for change? *Diversity and Democracy, 14*(3), 5–7.

Nagda, B. (R). A., & Gurin, P. (2007). Intergroup dialogue: A critical-dialogic approach to learning about difference, inequality, and social justice. In M. Kaplan & A. T. Miller (Eds.), *New Directions for Teaching and Learning: No. 111. Scholarship of multicultural teaching and learning* (pp. 35–45). San Francisco, CA: Jossey-Bass.

Nagda, B. (R). A., Gurin, P., Sorensen, N., & Zúñiga, X. (2009). Evaluating intergroup dialogue: Engaging diversity for personal and social responsibility. *Diversity & Democracy*, *12*(1), 4–6.

Nagda, B. (R). A., & Maxwell, K. E. (2011). Deepening the layers of understanding and connection: A critical-dialogic approach to facilitating intergroup dialogues. In K. E. Maxwell, B. (R). A. Nagda, M. C. Thompson, & P. Gurin (Eds.), *Facilitating intergroup dialogues: Bridging differences, catalyzing change* (pp. 1–22). Sterling, VA: Stylus Publishing.

National Center for Education Statistics. (n.d.). Fast facts. Retrieved from http://nces.ed.gov /fastfacts/display.asp?id=98.

National Geographic Education Foundation. (2006). *Final report: National Geographic-Roper Public Affairs: 2006 geographic literacy study*. Retrieved from http://www.nationalgeographic .com/roper2006/pdf/FINALReport2006GeogLitsurvey.pdf.

National Intergroup Dialogue Institute. (2015). Retrieved from https://igr.umich.edu/article /national-intergroup-dialogue-institute

National Science Foundation. (n.d.). *ADVANCE: Increasing the participation and advancement of women in academic science and engineering careers*. Retrieved from http://www.nsf.gov /funding/pgm_summ.jsp?pims_id=5383

Nelson Laird, T. F. (2005). College students' experiences with diversity and their effects on academic self-confidence, social agency, and disposition toward critical thinking. *Research in Higher Education, 46*(4), 365–387.

Nelson Laird, T. F. (2011). Measuring the diversity inclusivity of college courses. *Research in Higher Education, I*(6), 572–588.

Nelson Laird, T. F. (2014). Reconsidering the inclusion of diversity in the curriculum. *Diversity and Democracy, 17*(4), Retrieved from https://www.aacu.org/diversitydemocracy/2014 /fall/nelson-laird

Nelson Laird, T. F. N., & Engberg, M. E. (2011). Establishing differences between diversity requirements and other courses with varying degrees of diversity inclusivity. *Journal of General Education, 60*(2), 117–137.

Nettles, R., & Balter, R. (2012). *Multiple minority identities: Applications for practice, research, and training*. New York: Springer.

Neville, H., Spanierman, L., & Doan, B-T. (2006). Exploring the association between colorblind racial ideology and multicultural counseling competencies. *Cultural Diversity and Ethnic Minority Psychology, 12*(2), 275–290.

Niskode-Dossett, A. S., & John, E. A. (2015). Multiracial border work: Exploring the relationship between validation, student involvement, and epistemological development. In D. Mitchell Jr., K. M. Soria, E. A. Daniele, & J. A. Gipson (Eds.), *Student involvement and academic outcomes: Implications for diverse college student populations* (pp. 25–40). New York: Peter Lang Publishing.

Northern Illinois University. (2015). *Multicultural curriculum transformation: Office of the Provost*. Retrieved from http://www.niu.edu/mct/

Nunez, A-M., Hurtado, S., & Galdeano, E. C. (Eds.). (2015). *Hispanic-serving institutions: Advancing research and transformative practice*. New York: Routledge.

Oberlin College. (2015). *Mission*. Retrieved from http://new.oberlin.edu/about/mission.dot

Okoh, O., & de Sherbinin, J. (n.d.). *"Do this... ...not that": A shout-out from students of color to the faculty & staff at Colby College*. Unpublished pamphlet, Colby College.

Orfield, G. (2001). Introduction. In G. Orfield (with M. Kurlaender) (Eds.), *Diversity challenged: Evidence on the impact of affirmative action* (pp. 1–29). Cambridge, MA: Harvard Education Publishing Group.

Ortiz, A. M., & Santos, S. J. (2009). *Ethnicity in college: Advancing theory and improving diversity practices on campus*. Sterling, VA: Stylus Publishing

Pascarella, E. T. (2006). How college affects students: Ten directions for future research. *Journal of College Student Development, 47*(5), 508–520.

Pasquesi, K. (2013). Navigating difference through multicultural service learning. In S. K. Watt & J. L. Linley, *New Directions for Student Services: No. 144. Creating successful multicultural initiatives in higher education and student affairs* (pp. 37–45). San Francisco, CA: Jossey-Bass.

Perna, L. W. (2006). Studying college choice: A proposed conceptual model. In J. C. Smart (Ed.), *Higher education: Handbook of theory and research*, (Vol. 21, pp. 99–157). New York: Springer.

Peterson, M. W., & Spencer, M. G. (1990). Understanding academic culture and climate. In W. G. Tierney (Ed.), *Assessing academic climates and cultures* (pp. 3–18). San Francisco: Jossey-Bass.

Pettigrew, T. F. (2008). Future directions for intergroup contact theory and research. *International Journal of Intercultural Relations, 32*(3), 187–199.

Pettigrew, T. F., & Tropp, L. R. (2005). Allport's intergroup contact hypothesis: Its history and influence. In J. F. Dovidio, P. Glick, & L. A. Rudman (Eds.), *On the nature of prejudice: Fifty years after Allport* (pp. 262–277). Oxford, UK: Blackwell Publishing.

Pettigrew, T. F., & Tropp, L. R. (2006). A meta-analytic test of intergroup contact theory. *Journal of Personality and Social Psychology, 90*(5), 751–783.

Piaget, J. (1975/1985). *The equilibrium of cognitive structures: The central problem of intellectual development*. Chicago: University of Chicago Press.

Picca, L. H., & Feagin, J. R. (2007). *Two-faced racism: Whites in the backstage and frontstage*. New York: Routledge.

Pope, R., Reynolds, A. L., & Mueller, J. A. (2004). *Multicultural competence in student affairs*. San Francisco, CA: Jossey-Bass.

Powers, T. F. (2002). Postmodernism and James A. Banks's multiculturalism: The limits of intellectual history. *Educational Theory, 52*(2), 209–221.

Rankin, S. R. (2003). *Campus climate for gay, lesbian, bisexual, and transgender people: A national perspective*. Cambridge, MA: Policy Institute of the National Gay & Lesbian Task Force. Retrieved from http://www.thetaskforce.org/static_html/downloads/reports/reports/CampusClimate.pdf.

Rankin, S. R., & Reason, R. D. (2005). Differing perceptions: How students of color and white students perceive campus climate for underrepresented groups. *Journal of College Student Development, 46*(1), 43–61.

Reason, R. D., & Watson, K. T. (2011). Multicultural competence and social justice advocacy. In D. L. Stewart (Ed.), *Multicultural student services on campus: Building bridges, re-visioning community* (pp. 267–281). Sterling, VA: Stylus Publishing.

Renn, K. A. (2000). Patterns of situational identity among biracial and multiracial college students. *Review of Higher Education, 23*(4), 399–420.

Renn, K. A. (2003). Understanding the identities of mixed-race college students through a developmental ecology lens. *Journal of College Student Development, 44*(3), 383–403.

Renn, K. A. (2004). *Mixed race students in college: The ecology of race, identity, and community on campus.* Albany, NY: State University of New York.

Renn, K. A., & Arnold, K. D. (2003). Reconceptualizing research on college student peer culture. *Journal of Higher Education, 74*(3), 261–291.

Reynolds, A. L., & Pope, R. L. (1991). The complexities of diversity: Exploring multiple oppressions. *Journal of Counseling and Development, 70*(1), 174–180.

Reynolds-Keefer, L., Peet, M. R., Gurin, P., & Lonn, S. (2011). *Fostering integrative knowledge and lifelong learning.* Retrieved from http://www.aacu.org/peerreview/2011-2012/fall-winter/fostering-integrative-learning

Rhoads, R. A. (1994). *Coming out in college: The struggle for a queer identity.* Westport, CT: Bergin & Garvey.

Rhoads, R. A., & Valadez, J. R. (1996). *Democracy, multiculturalism, and the community college: A critical perspective.* New York: Garland Publishing.

Rogers, G., Holloway, A., & Priddy, L. (2014). *Exploring degree qualifications: A descriptive analysis of the quality initiative demonstration project to test the Lumina Foundation's Degree Qualifications Profile.* Chicago, IL: Higher Learning Commission. Retrieved from http://www.learningoutcomeassessment.org/documents/HLCFinalReport.pdf

Roscigno, V. J., & Wilson, G. (2014). The relational foundations of inequality at work I: Status, interaction, and culture. *American Behavioral Scientist, 58*, 219–227.

Ross, F. E. (2005). *Achieving cultural competence: The role of mentoring in sexual minority identity development* (Unpublished doctoral dissertation). Indiana University.

Rynes, S. L. (2007). Let's create a tipping point: What academics and practitioners can do, alone and together. *Academy of Management Journal, 50*(5), 1046–1054.

Sahlins, M. (1976). *The use and abuse of biology: An anthropological critique of sociobiology.* Ann Arbor: University of Michigan.

San Diego State University (SDSU). (n.d.). Cultural competency certificate program: A commitment to diversity. Retrieved from http://go.sdsu.edu/education/cultural-competence-certificate-students.aspx

Schein, E. H. (2010). *Organizational culture and leadership.* San Francisco, CA: Jossey-Bass.

Schneider, B., & Barbera, K. (2014). Introduction: The Oxford handbook of organizational climate and culture. In B. Schneider and K. Barbera (Eds.), *The Oxford handbook of organizational climate and culture* (pp. 3–22). New York: Oxford University Press.

Schneider, C. G. (2010). Foreword. In E. L. Dey, M. C. Ott, M. Antonaros, C. L. Barnhardt, & M. A. Holsapple (Ed.), *Engaging diverse viewpoints: What is the campus climate for perspective-taking?* (pp. ix–xi). Washington, DC: Association of American Colleges and Universities. Retrieved from https://www.aacu.org/sites/default/files/files/core_commitments/engaging_diverse_viewpoints.pdf

Schneider, C. G. (2015). Foreword. In. P. L. Gaston (Ed.), *General education transformed: How we can, why we must* (pp. v–ix). Washington, DC: Association of American Colleges and Universities.

Schwartz, M. P. (2010). *How diverse are governing boards? How diverse should they be?* Retrieved from http://agb.org/trusteeship/2010/novemberdecember/how-diverse-are-governing-boar ds-how-diverse-should-they-be

Sherwin, J. (2011). Competency-based medical education takes shape. *AAMC Reporter*. Retrieved from http://tulane.edu/som/ome/upload/Competency-Based-Medical-Education-Takes-Shape-AAMC.docx

Sidanius, J., Levin, S., Van Laar, C., & Sears, D. O. (2008). *The diversity challenge: Social identity and intergroup relations on the college campus.* New York: Russell Sage Foundation.

Smith, D. G. (1990). Embracing diversity as a central campus goal. *Academe, 76*(6), 29–33.

Smith, D. G. (2004). *The campus diversity initiative: Current status, anticipating the future.* Retrieved from http://cgu.edu/PDFFiles/CDIStatusandFuture2004.pdf

Smith, D. G., & Parker, S. (2005). Organizational learning: A tool for diversity and institutional effectiveness. In A. J. Kezar (Ed.), *Organizational learning in higher education* (pp. 113–125). San Francisco: Jossey-Bass.

Smith, D. G., & Wolf-Wendel, L. E. (2005). The challenge of diversity: Involvement or alienation in the academy? [*ASHE-ERIC Higher Education Report*, 31(1)]. San Francisco, CA: Jossey-Bass.

Smith, S., Prohn, S., Driscoll, L., Hesterberg, D., Bradley, L., & Grossman, J. (2014). Preparing students for a diverse future: Using service-learning for career training in soil science community outreach. *NACTA Journal, 58*(4), 293–301.

Sorensen, N., Nagda, B. (R). A., Gurin, P., & Maxwell, K. E. (2009). Taking a "hands on" approach to diversity in higher education: A critical-dialogic model for effective intergroup interaction. *Analyses of Social Issues and Public Policy, 9*(1), 3–35.

Spitzberg, B., & Changnon, G. (2009). Conceptualizing intercultural competence. In D. K. Deardorff (Ed.), *The SAGE handbook of intercultural competence* (pp. 2–52). Thousand Oaks, CA: SAGE Publications.

Stanley, C. A., Saunders, S., & Hart, J. M. (2005). Multicultural course transformation. In M. L. Ouellett (Ed.): *Teaching inclusively: Resources for course, department and institutional change in higher education* (pp. 566–585). Stillwater, OK: New Forums Press.

Steenbarger, B. N. (1991). All the world is not a stage: Emerging contextualist themes in counseling and development. *Journal of Counseling & Development, 70*(2), 288–296.

Steinberg, S. R., & Kincheloe, J. L. (2009). Smoke and mirrors: More than one way to be diverse and multicultural. In S. R. Steinberg (Ed.): *Diversity and multiculturalism: A reader* (pp. 3–22). New York: Peter Lang.

Strange, C. C., & Banning, J. H. (2001). *Educating by design: Creating campus learning environments that work.* San Francisco, CA: Jossey-Bass.

Suchman, M. C. (1995). Managing legitimacy: Strategic and institutional approaches. *Academy of Management Review, 20*(3), 571–610.

Sue, D. W., Arredondo, P., & McDavis, R. J. (1992). Multicultural competencies/standards: A pressing need. *Journal of Counseling and Development, 70*, 477–486.

Sue, D. W., Carter, R. T., Casas, J. M., Fouad, N. A., Ivey, A. E., Jensen, M., LaFromboise, T., ... Vazquez-Nutall, E. (1998). *Multicultural counseling competencies: Individual and organizational development.* Thousand Oaks, CA: SAGE Publications.

Sue, D. W., & Sue, D. (2013). *Counseling the culturally diverse: Theory and practice* (6th ed.). Hoboken, NJ: John Wiley & Sons, Inc.

Svrluga, S. (2015, March 27). OU: Frat members learned racist chant at national SAE leadership event. *Washington Post*. Retrieved from http://www.washingtonpost.com/news/gradepoint/wp/2015/03/27/ou-investigation-sae-members-learned-racist-chant-at-national-leadership-event/

Swartz, D. (1997). *Culture and power: The sociology of Pierre Bourdieu*. Chicago: University of Chicago.

Tatum, B. D. (1992). Talking about race, learning about racism: The application of racial identity development theory in the classroom. *Harvard Educational Review, 62*(1), 1–24.

Tatum, B. D. (1997). *Why are all the black kids sitting together in the cafeteria: And other conversations about race*. New York: Basic Books. 01

Taylor, P. (2014). *The next America*. Retrieved from http://www.pewresearch.org/next-america/

Tierney, W. G. (1999). Models of minority college-going and retention: Cultural integrity versus cultural suicide. *Journal of Negro Education, 68*(1), 80–91.

Tinto, V. (1988). Stages of student departure: Reflections on the longitudinal character of student leaving. *Journal of Higher Education, 59*(4), 438–455.

Torres, V., Howard-Hamilton, M. F., & Cooper, D. L. (2003). Identity development of diverse populations: Implications for teaching and administration in higher education [*ASHE-ERIC Higher Education Report, 29*(6)]. San Francisco, CA: Jossey-Bass.

Tropp, L. R., & Pettigrew, T. F. (2005). Differential relationships between intergroup contact and affective and cognitive dimensions of prejudice. *Personality & Social Psychology Bulletin, 31*(8), 1145–1158.

Tuchman, G. (2009). *Wannabe U: Inside the corporate university*. Chicago: University of Chicago Press.

Twombly, S. B., Salisbury, M. H., Tumanut, S. D., & Klute, P. (2012). Study abroad in a new global century: Renewing the promise, refining the purpose [*ASHE-ERIC Higher Education Report, 38*(4)]. San Francisco, CA: Jossey-Bass.

University of Colorado at Colorado Springs. (n.d.). *Our commitment to the future: 2012–2020 strategic plan*. Retrieved from http://www.uccs.edu/Documents/chancellor/strategic%20plans/Approved%20Strategic%20Plan/uccs-strategic-plan-2012-2020.pdf

University of Maryland. (2014). *Mission and goals statement: University of Maryland, College Park*. Retrieved from http://www.provost.umd.edu/Strategic_Planning/UMCP_Mission_Statement-Final-submitted-29Apr2014.pdf

University of Maryland. (n.d.). *General Education @UMD*. Retrieved from http://gened.umd.edu/

University of Missouri. (2015). *Update on a proposal for a diversity requirement*. Retrieved from https://transparency.missouri.edu/2015/10/21/15/

University of Washington. (2014). *About the UW School of Law: Leaders for the global common good*. (2014). Retrieved from http://www.law.washington.edu/about/

Unzueta, M. M., & Lowery, B. S. (2008). Defining racism safely: The role of self-image maintenance on white Americans' conceptions of racism. *Journal of Experimental Social Psychology, 44*(6), 1491–1497.

Vandiver, B. J., Cross, W. E. Jr., Worrell, F. C., & Fhagen-Smith, P. E. (2002). Validating the cross racial identity scale. *Journal of Counseling Psychology, 49*(1), 71–85.

Van de Vijver, F. J. R., & Leung, K. (2009). Methodological issues in researching intercultural competence. In D. K. Deardorff (Ed.), *The SAGE handbook of intercultural competence* (pp. 404–418). Thousand Oaks, CA: SAGE Publications.

Vogelgesang, L. J., & Astin, A. W. (2000). Comparing the effects of community service and service-learning. *Michigan Journal of Community Service Learning, 7*(1), 25–34.

Ward, K. (1995). Service learning in honors education: Involving students in citizenship and social change. *The National Honors Report, 16*, 45–46.

Ward, K. (2003). Faculty service roles and the scholarship of engagement [*ASHE-ERIC Higher Education Report*, 29(5)]. San Francisco, CA: Jossey-Bass.

Ward, K., & Wolf-Wendel, L. (2000). Community-centered service learning: Moving from doing for to doing with. *American Behavioral Scientist, 43*, 767–780.

Ward, K. M., & Zarate, M. E. (2015). The influence of campus racial climate on graduate student attitudes about the benefits of diversity. *Review of Higher Education, 38*(4), 589–617.

WASC Senior College and University Commission (WSCUC). (2013). *2013 handbook of accreditation revised.* Retrieved from http://www.wascsenior.org/resources/handbook-accreditation-2013

Weah, W., Simmons, V. C., & Hall, M. (2000). Service-learning and multicultural/multiethnic perspectives: From diversity to equity. *Phi Delta Kappan, 81*(9), 673–675.

Wijeyesinghe, C. L. (2001). Racial identity in multiracial people: An alternative paradigm. In C. L. Wijeyesinghe & B. W. Jackson (Eds.), *New perspectives on racial identity development: A theoretical and practical anthology* (pp. 129–152). New York: New York University Press.

Williams, D. (2006). Overcoming the brutal facts: Building and implementing a relentless diversity change process. *The Diversity Factor, 14*(4), 10–18.

Williams, D. A. (2013). *Strategic diversity leadership: Activating change and transformation in higher education.* Sterling, VA: Stylus.

Williams, D. A., Berger, J. B., & McClendon, S. A. (2005). *Toward a model of inclusive excellence and change in postsecondary institutions.* Washington, DC: Association of American Colleges and Universities. Retrieved from http://aacu.org/sites/default/files/files/mei/williams_et_al.pdf

Williams, D. A., & Wade-Golden, K. C. (2013). *The chief diversity officer: Strategy structure, and change management.* Sterling, VA: Stylus.

Winkle-Wagner, R. (2010). Cultural capital: The promises and pitfalls in education research [*ASHE-ERIC Higher Education Report*, 36(1)]. San Francisco, CA: Jossey-Bass.

Yancy, G., & Feagin, J. (2015, July 27). American racism in the "white frame." *New York Times.* Retrieved from http://opinionator.blogs.nytimes.com/2015/07/27/american-racism-in-the-white-frame/?_r=1

Yeado, J. (2013). *Intentionally successful improving minority student college graduation rates.* Washington, DC: Education Trust. Retrieved from http://edtrust.org/wp-content/uploads/2013/10/Intentionally_Successful.pdf

Young, I. M. (1990). *Justice and the politics of difference.* Princeton University Press.

Zakaria, F. (2015). *In defense of a liberal education.* New York: W. W. Norton & Company.

Zhao, C-M., & Kuh, G. D. (2004). Adding value: Learning communities and student engagement. *Research in Higher Education, 45*(2), 115–138.

Zúñiga, X., Nagda, B. (R). A., Chesler, M., & Cytron-Walker, A. (2007). Intergroup dialogue in higher education: Meaningful learning about social justice [*ASHE-ERIC Higher Education Report*, 32(4)]. Hoboken, NJ: Wiley.

Appendix A: Data Sample

Written Survey Sample

Forty-three college graduates who had completed a 4-year baccalaureate degree within the last 15 years completed the contact information and answered most or all of the questions in an online written survey. The demographics of the written survey participants included 27 females and 13 males, with 3 who did not identify gender. The sample included 27 whites, 7 black or African Americans, 4 Asians or Asian Americans, 1 American Indian white, 2 Asian whites, and 2 African-American whites. Of the sample, 37 individuals self-identified as heterosexual, 4 as lesbian/gay, 1 as bisexual and 1 as pansexual.

The survey sample reflected baccalaureate graduates from 20 different institutions including 12 from private liberal arts colleges; 13 from public doctoral research universities and 1 from a private doctoral research university; 13 from public colleges including 2 from historically black colleges; and 2 from private undergraduate universities. Geographic areas represented include 24 graduates of institutions in the Midwest, 11 in the East, 5 in the South, and 3 in the West. Since contact was made with a number of professors at specific institutions to request that they contact recent graduates, the sample included 13 participants from a single Midwestern public college, 4 from a Midwestern doctoral research university, and 4 from an Eastern private liberal arts college.

The range of majors in the sample include 21 from scientific disciplines with 11 in biology, 7 in psychology, 1 in neuroscience, 1 in marine sciences and 1 in chemistry; 7 in the social sciences including 4 in sociology and 3 in government/political science; 6 in the humanities with 5 in English and 1 in religion; 4 in women's studies; 3 in business/finance, and 1 each in music and journalism.

On average, the 43 participants rated the responsiveness of campus culture for diversity as slightly above 4 on a scale of 1 to 5. Although 37 of the participants in the sample had taken diversity-related coursework as undergraduates, only 15 indicated that the coursework was part of a general education requirement. A number of the graduates could not remember the titles of the course(s) they had taken. Thirty-three respondents indicated that other courses they had taken included diversity-related content, whereas 32 indicated that they had taken courses that discussed America's racial history or contemporary racial/ethnic issues. Thirty-five responded that the courses they took had strengthened their diversity competency. In addition, 25 participants stated that they had engaged in cocurricular activities or programs that strengthened their understanding of diverse populations.

Interview Sample

Of the 43 participants in the written survey, 25 graduates indicated a willingness to be interviewed, but after one or more email attempts, contact could be made with only 17 of these individuals. The interview sample was diverse and included 7 males and 10 females as well as 11 whites, 3 African Americans, 1 Asian, and 2 Asian whites. In addition, the interview sample included one participant who self-identified as gay/lesbian, one as pansexual, and one as bisexual.

The interviews were conducted over the telephone and each interview lasted from 30 minutes to 1 hour. Before each interview, informed consent was obtained to record the interview and the participants were provided with the transcribed passages selected for publication for their review and consent. The interviews used several vignettes adapted from scenarios in the research literature to elicit interviewee feedback in addition to a number of open-ended questions.

Name Index

Subject Index

A

Academic Quality Improvement Program (AQIP), 106

Academic service learning, 99–102. *See also* Educational terrain mapping

Allport's contact theory, 102–103

Allport's intergroup contact theory, 122

American Association of State Colleges and Universities, 64

Asian Pacific American (APA), 101

Association of American Colleges and Universities (AAC&U), 23, 27, 78, 79, 83

B

Banks' theory, sociopolitical implications of, 39

C

Campus Conversations on Race (CCOR), 125

Campus Diversity Initiative (CDI), 70

Campus ecology, 111; component of, 65

Campus environment, ecological model application to, 55–56. *See also* Diversity competence, ecological framework for

Campus racial climate, 63

Chronosystem, 55

Committee on Multicultural Curriculum Transformation (CMCT), 97

Communicative synchrony, 37

Competence based medical education (CBME), 43

Competence, defined, 18

Cultural bubble, 22

Cultural competence, 18; deconstructing, 32–34, 48–49; diversity competence, 44–45; diversity/cultural competence, 46–48; intercultural competence, 34–37; multicultural competence, 37–40; rethinking culture, 40–43; unbundling competence, 43–44; multidimensional model for, 40; pathway to, 27–29; *See also* Higher education, politics of cultural competence in

Cultural competency activities, 101

Cultural integration, 64–65

Culturally Engaging Campus Environments (CECE), 30, 59, 111, 132

Cultural pluralism, 76

D

Degree Qualifications Profile (DQP), 106

"Democratic microcosms," 68

Diverse Learning Environments (DLE), 60

Diversity competence: ecological framework for, 50–53, 71–72; campus culture and climate, 62–65; campus diversity experiences, 53–54; campus physical environment, 65–66; diversity

About the Authors

Edna Chun and **Alvin Evans** are award-winning authors and human resources (HR) and diversity leaders, each over two decades of experience in higher education. Two of their books, *Are the Walls Really Down? Behavioral and Organizational Barriers to Faculty and Staff Diversity* (Jossey-Bass, 2007) and *Bridging the Diversity Divide: Globalization and Reciprocal Empowerment in Higher Education* (Jossey-Bass, 2009), are recipients of the prestigious Kathryn G. Hansen Publication Award by the national College and University Professional Association for Human Resources.

Their most recent publication, *Affirmative Action at a Crossroads: Fisher and Forward* (2015) offers viable strategies that maximize the educational benefits of diversity in light of recent Supreme Court decisions and is a helpful companion to the current monograph. Their coauthored book, *The Department Chair as Transformative Diversity Leader: Building Inclusive Learning Environments in Higher Education* (Stylus, 2014), is the first book to provide a research-based, approach to the chair's diversity leadership role in the academic department.

Other recent publications include *Diverse Administrators in Peril: The New Indentured Class in Higher Education* (Paradigm, 2012), the first in-depth examination of the work experiences of minority, female, and lesbian, gay, bisexual, and transgender administrators in higher education. Two additional books explore the role of human resource and diversity talent strategies: *Creating a Tipping Point: Strategic Human Resources in Higher Education*

(Jossey Bass, 2012), a research-based approach to the development of strategic HR talent management practices in higher education, and *The New Talent Acquisition Frontier: Integrating HR and Diversity Strategy in the Private and Public Sectors and Higher Education* (Stylus, 2014). The latter received a silver medal in the 2014 Axiom Business Book Awards and is the first book to provide a concrete road map to the integration of HR and diversity strategy.

Evans and Chun have published a number of journal articles in leading HR, diversity, and academic publications and are frequent presenters at national conferences and symposia. Edna Chun is chief learning officer and Alvin Evans serves as higher education practice leader for HigherEd Talent, a national HR and diversity consulting firm.

About the ASHE Higher Education Report Series

Since 1983, the ASHE (formerly ASHE-ERIC) Higher Education Report Series has been providing researchers, scholars, and practitioners with timely and substantive information on the critical issues facing higher education. Each monograph presents a definitive analysis of a higher education problem or issue, based on a thorough synthesis of significant literature and institutional experiences. Topics range from planning to diversity and multiculturalism, to performance indicators, to curricular innovations. The mission of the Series is to link the best of higher education research and practice to inform decision making and policy. The reports connect conventional wisdom with research and are designed to help busy individuals keep up with the higher education literature. Authors are scholars and practitioners in the academic community. Each report includes an executive summary, review of the pertinent literature, descriptions of effective educational practices, and a summary of key issues to keep in mind to improve educational policies and practice.

This series is one of the most peer reviewed in higher education. A National Advisory Board made up of ASHE members reviews proposals. A National Review Board of ASHE scholars and practitioners reviews completed manuscripts. Six monographs are published each year, and they are approximately 144 pages in length. The reports are widely disseminated through Jossey-Bass and John Wiley & Sons, and they are available online to subscribing institutions through Wiley Online Library (http://wileyonlinelibrary.com).

Call for Proposals

The ASHE Higher Education Report Series is actively looking for proposals. We encourage you to contact one of the editors, Dr. Kelly Ward (kaward@wsu.edu) or Dr. Lisa Wolf-Wendel (lwolf@ku.edu), with your ideas.

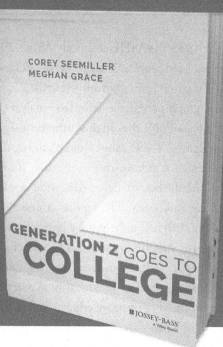